D1298470

Yale Center for British Art

SELECTED PAINTINGS
DRAWINGS & BOOKS

with a foreword by PAUL MELLON
Yale College Class of 1929

Published on the occasion of the inauguration
of the YALE CENTER FOR BRITISH ART
Yale University, New Haven, Connecticut
April 15, 1977

Copyright © 1977 by Yale University
All rights reserved
Library of Congress Catalog Card Number 77–71659

PREFACE

The collection of British art assembled by Paul Mellon over the last twenty years is one of the most comprehensive representations of the visual arts of a single culture ever brought together. As of this writing, the collection includes approximately seventeen hundred paintings, seven thousand drawings, five thousand prints, sixteen thousand rare books, and a small, representative group of sculptures. The holdings provide a survey of the development of British art and printing from the late fifteenth century to the middle of the nineteenth century. Its special emphasis lies in the period between the birth of Hogarth (1697) and the death of Turner (1851), considered by many to be the "golden age" of English art. Among the collection's highlights are such individual works as Van Dyck's *Earl of Newport*, William Hogarth's *The Beggar's Opera*, Richard Wilson's *A View of Rome from the Villa Madonna*, Constable's *Hadleigh Castle*, and Turner's *View of Dordrecht;* the watercolors by Turner and Blake; the thirteen examples of the earliest English printing by William Caxton; and the color-plate books from the J. R. Abbey Collection. In addition to these works there are large holdings in particular areas of interest. The numerous Wrights of Derby, the incomparable Stubbs collection, the small portraits by Gainsborough, Zoffany and Devis, the fine examples of sporting art, the Elizabethan and Jacobean portraits, the English Canalettos and van de Veldes, the interesting small Claude de Jongh *The Thames at Westminster Stairs*—give the collection an overall richness and strength that only a very few institutions in England can boast. The lack of emphasis in areas like that of formal portraiture—popular among an earlier generation of American collectors—and academic history painting is less apparent than one would expect: the collection possesses the fine Reynolds full-length of *Charles Stanhope, 3rd Earl of Harrington*, the Romney *John Flaxman Modelling the Bust of William Hayley*, and the important Fuseli *Death of Dido*. The collection also includes a small but valuable group of portrait miniatures, many rare panoramas and atlases, and some nineteenth century toys. In all, it is a treasure providing resources for both study and delectation. As such, it is ideally suited for an institution whose function will be to make the visual resources of a single culture enjoyed and understood within the context of not only art history, but also history, literature, and possibly other areas of study.

In the Foreword of this publication, Mr. Mellon has charted the development of the collection. And the growth of the collection between 1959 and 1963 can only be described as astounding. Subsequently the collection has grown more selectively, and among the more recent acquisitions have been the great Turner masterpiece *Dort*, Joseph Wright of Derby's *The Blacksmith's Shop* and *An Academy by Lamplight*, the lovely Reynolds *Mrs. Abington*, Hogarth's *John Palmer*, and the Rubens *Allegory of Peace and Plenty*. This evolution in Mr. Mellon's collecting is a natural one and has helped to refine and strengthen the collection in many areas.

We wish to thank Mr. Mellon for kindly allowing us to reprint in the Foreword excerpts from his speech delivered on the occasion of the opening of the exhibition of his collection in The Virginia Museum of Fine Arts in 1963. These words and the remarks about the development of the collection in more recent years provide a better introduction to the collection than any further statement that can be made about it. Moreover, they provide an insight into the strong feelings and motivations underlying the endeavor, which have played a critical role in determining both the scope and fine quality of the objects acquired.

Thanks are also due to those responsible for this publication, in particular to the three senior curators and their staffs who took valuable time away from their other duties to select the illustrations and write the accompanying commentaries for works in their departments: Malcolm Cormack, Curator of Paintings; Joan Friedman, Curator of Rare Books; and Andrew Wilton, Curator of Prints and Drawings. Beverly Carter and Mary Ann Thompson, of Mr. Mellon's staff, also deserve a special word of thanks for their efforts in locating objects and supplying badly needed information about them. The photography was carried out by Joseph Szaszfai and David Holbrook; the editing and preparation of the manuscript were done by Elise K. Kenney and Lynne Silkman; and the design and production supervision were executed by Howard Gralla of the Yale University Printing Service.

Without the help of all of these individuals as well as others of the Center staff this publication would not have been possible.

EDMUND P. PILLSBURY
Director

A COLLECTOR RECOLLECTS
by Paul Mellon

Excerpts from a speech delivered at the opening of the exhibition "Painting in England 1700–1850" at The Virginia Museum of Fine Arts, Richmond, April 20, 1963, and remarks about the development of the collection in more recent years.

The first painting that I can remember was on the walls of my family's house in Pittsburgh. It was the charming portrait by Romney of the little girl, Miss Willoughby, now in our National Gallery. As you know, my father was a collector of paintings before me, and at that time (roughly just before and during World War I), his interests were mainly in the Dutch 17th century and English 18th century Schools (although there were a few Barbizon painters represented, two Corots, a large Troyon, a Cazin, and some others). There were one or two English landscapes, and about ten of those formal portraits, large and small, which we in America have come to associate English art with almost exclusively—those of Gainsborough, Reynolds, Lawrence, Hoppner, Romney, Raeburn.

The house was late Victorian and very dark—the halls were dark, the walls were dark, and outside, Pittsburgh itself was *very* dark. John Walker, former Director of our National Gallery, and an old friend and fellow-Pittsburgher, describes my father's collection by saying, "His views of Holland and England opened windows on a world more attractive than the atmosphere of Pittsburgh, where at night every aperture was covered with cheesecloth and all the furniture draped in sheets to keep out the constantly settling soot."

Now I don't really remember it as being *quite* as bad as that, but perhaps it was, and only my memory and modern efforts at smoke-control have made Pittsburgh more acceptable. In any case, these very urbane and always self-confident personages in their classical landscapes and autumnal parklands smiled down at me with what seemed a warm and friendly glow. My father was not much of a conversationalist, but he did occasionally talk about a painting he liked, and you got the feeling that he did really like them; that they meant, in fact, a great deal to him.

My mother was English. From 1907 until 1914, from my first year to my seventh, my parents spent almost every summer in England, and my sister and I were invariably taken with them. I suppose it was in those summers that I first developed a taste for the English countryside, for English houses, English rivers, English parks, English skies, English clouds—and let's not forget English trains—in those days brilliantly and beautifully painted in reds, greens, or blues; all the brass and copper which garnished the engines highly polished, all the engines proudly and aristocratically named. Perhaps it was the joy of rushing through the countryside in those beautiful trains that first gave me the love of the countryside; but I prefer to think it was the beauty of the countryside itself that brought me, and my parents, onto the trains! From those distant summers I remember huge dark trees in rolling parks, herds of small friendly deer, flotillas of white swans on the Thames, dappled tan cows in soft green fields, the grey mass of Windsor Castle towering in the distance against a background of huge golden summer clouds; soldiers in scarlet and bright metal, drums and bugles, troops of grey horses; laughing ladies in white with gay parasols, men in impeccable white flannels and striped blazers, and always behind them and behind everything the grass was green, green, green. Of course, there were ominous happenings, the awesome talk of grownups, gathering clouds, then as now—the sinking of the Titanic, rumors of war, the antics of the suffragettes. There were also the small annoyances—the constant staccato of punctures and blowouts on even the shortest of automobile excursions. But somehow at this great distance it all melts into a sunny and imperturbable English summer landscape. There seemed to be a tranquility in those days that has never again been found, and a quietness as detached from life as the memory itself.

The war came, we stayed at home, Pittsburgh stayed dark and sooty, the paintings still shone. We went to Washington in 1921, and most of the paintings went with us. I went away to school, and then from 1925 to 1929, on to Yale. While there I had the unrepeatable and unforgettable privilege of studying under, and hearing the lectures of, and making friends with, several of the great Yale teachers of the day—Chauncey Tinker in the Age of Johnson, Billy Phelps in Tennyson and Browning, Bob French in the Age of Chaucer, John Allison in the Middle Ages. And there were others. They all confirmed my predilection for things English and for things old, and although art in those days was not my major study, nor my major interest, I am sure these men helped to sharpen my eyes and ears to enlarge my enjoyment and comprehension of the beauty in art as well as in nature. They also pushed me further over the brink into a state of galloping Anglophilia—or perhaps I should say, I turned into a galloping Anglophile.

For my next educational venture was Cambridge, which involved quite a lot of galloping. There I hunted with the Fitzwilliam regularly, occasionally with the Quorn, the Belvoir, and the Pytchley. I rowed regularly in non-hunting seasons in our college boat on the Cam, and I even learned to navigate a punt. Once again, I thoroughly enjoyed living in England: and I drank deeply of her scenery, her history, her life, her sport, her beer. I went to lectures, but Tinker and Phelps had spoiled me, and I found Cambridge lectures dull and dry. I read a little, I studied a little, I finally received a B.A. Honors Degree, although what class (I, II, or III) is highly classified information! In other words, I r-o-d-e constantly, I r-o-w-e-d intermittently, I r-e-a-d a little. But Cambridge I loved, and I loved its grey walls, its grassy quadrangles, St. Mary's bells, its busy, narrow streets, full of men in black gowns, King's Chapel and Choir and candlelight, the coal-fire smell, and walking across the quadrangle in a dressing gown in the rain to take a bath. In the winter, it got dark at 3:30, and all winter the wet wind whistled straight down from the North Sea—and on grey days or sunny days, the flat, wide, seemingly unpeopled, limitless fields stretched endlessly away to the north across the mysterious fens. To the east they rolled gently toward Suffolk and lovely Newmarket, its long straight velvet training gallops, its race-course, to me the most beautiful one anywhere. To the south and west, toward London and life and the real world.

While I was at Cambridge, and a year later while I occasionally stayed in London with my father during his Ambassadorship, I began collecting books, particularly English color-plate books and books on racing and hunting (another unfortunate and expensive habit I have never been able to break). From the Robinson Brothers in Pall Mall, I bought my first illustrated sporting book in 1931—Strutt's *Sports and Pastimes of the People of England*. Later, after I was first married in 1935, and until World War II, I began buying racing and hunting and other sporting paintings, such as the lively Ben Marshall of *Thomas Mellish*, and the charming Stubbs portrait of the Racehorse *Pumpkin*. I was able also, in many of those years, to get in a month or so of hunting and riding in point-to-points. My father gave me two of my best Ben Marshalls and two Sartoriuses as wedding presents, although he detested hunting as being very dangerous and racing as being very foolish, and he often said, "Any damn fool knows one horse can run faster than another." It was, however, at about this very time that I bought my first racehorse (an interesting commentary on the influence of parental advice)!

After World War II, in the late Forties (my early forties), I continued in a desultory way to collect English pictures and books, both here and abroad. We had moved to Virginia just before the war, and had built a rather large Georgian house. It was a house that later proved too large for living in but too small for our subsequent family of four children—large hallways and living rooms, and high ceilings, but very few bedrooms. It was more formal and institutional than personal and liveable, and we soon moved out to a smaller but more roomy farmhouse. The big, or Brick House, as it is now called, has recently been called back into service to house this Collection, and to house most of my English books, and it has proved very useful and appropriate for the purpose. While living there we acquired more sporting paintings, as well as the attractive and comprehensive collection of English color-plate books illustrative of the Scenery of England, Life in England, and Travel in England and the Continent, which had been formed by Major John Abbey. We had also slowly been building up a collection of books by, and illustrated by, William Blake. And the Sporting Library was gradually being added to, as well.

I hasten to absolve my wife, Bunny, from whatever blame our critics might level at this Collection—many of the paintings, perhaps the larger and wilder and less aesthetically attractive ones (like the hungry Stubbs Lion, or like the more obviously historical and documentary paintings, which she would never have bought on her own). In such matters she defers to Basil Taylor's and my own crazy tastes and ideas! But I believe I reflect her sentiments correctly when I say that on the whole she shares equally my enthusiasm for English art, as one who appreciates true art in any form, and as one who loves the country, architecture, flowers, gardens, and trees. As one who, I might say, is a brilliant artist in her own right in the fields of land-scaping, gardening and architecture.

Only a small fraction of our English Collection, however, (and I speak of paintings, not books) was assembled before 1959. In that year, in London, through my activities as Chairman of the *Sport and the Horse* Committee of the Virginia Museum, I met Basil Taylor, art historian and critic, who was then an official of the Royal College of Art. Through our discussions about English pictures for that show, and through other talks and correspondence about English art, we developed a kind of partnership arrangement which has always seemed to me completely delightful and unique. Knowing of my interest, sensing my enthusiasm, and perceiving my frustration at being thousands of miles from the main sources of British art—the London dealers and the London auctions—he agreed to represent me in an unofficial, unpublicized, and I am quick to say, uncompensated capacity. His scholarship, his knowledge of English art, his familiarity with and access to the sources, his expert knowledge and long experience, made his arduous and devoted activity in searching out and expertizing paintings an invaluable asset to me and to the Collection.

Our correspondence was voluminous and often very funny. Photographs and transparencies, to say nothing of real drawings and paintings, shuttled across the Atlantic by the boatload and planeload—and the overseas telephone knew no rest. In general, I accepted most of Basil Taylor's recommendations because I responded enthusiastically to them. In other words, there was a general and most satisfactory concurrence of taste between us. Occasionally, he persuaded me that a chance find or a personal choice of mine should be excluded for reasons of physical condition or doubtful attribution. Occasionally, I rejected his suggestions because of a dislike of a subject or an artist. (For some unaccountable reason, for instance, neither Bunny nor I can abide windmills in paintings. And I myself put a strict limit on the number of cows! Three is enough in any painting.) But on the whole our reactions, our enthusiasms, and our dislikes are remarkably similar. Needless to say, I acknowledge with sincere thanks that whatever knowledge of the field I have gained, that whatever discrimination I may have been able to develop, whatever the improvement in my "English eye"—is due to Basil.

It was he also who opened up my eyes to the beauty and freshness of English drawings and water-colors, their immediacy and sureness of technique, their comprehensiveness of subject matter, their vital qualities, their Englishness.

Since we had the encouragement of his enthusiasm as well as our own, since we had his invaluable advice and help, since we had the financial resources as well as the prospect of many years of personal enjoyment of our acquisitions, the main corpus of the Collection of paintings and water-colors materialized quickly.

I don't believe many motives in life are clearcut or self-evident. Collecting especially is such a matter of time and chance—intellectual bent, individual temperament, personal taste, available resources, changing fashion—and the psychologists tell us, even very early child-training—and my own motives as a collector seem to myself extremely mixed. Although temperamental trends or subjective impulses were perhaps uppermost, I won't say it was done entirely without thought, without reason, without plan. English Art, as well as being personally desirable, seemed to me long neglected or even abandoned, not only in this country but also in its homeland.

So that expanding the Collection, increasing its breadth and depth, filling in important historical or chronological gaps as well as adding artists and schools in which we were weak, or which we lacked entirely—all seemed part of a logical, deliberate attempt to say to ourselves and to the public—*this* is English Art, not just the *Duchess of Devonshire*, or the *Age of Innocence*; let's take it seriously, let's reevaluate it, let's look at it, let's enjoy it.

Here is an English tree, therefore, transplanted to Virginia soil. It has grown from a sapling almost too rapidly, perhaps, to have gained full strength or stature—it may grow new branches, brighter leaves, as time goes on. It may even require in the future a certain amount of judicious pruning. But far beyond the confines of this Collection and exhibition, I hope the high qualities and charming attributes of English Art will more and more be enjoyed throughout the Western World, and that the pleasure inherent in it, and its beneficent influence, will gradually become better and better known.

I don't know if I've answered any questions; or if I've said too much or too little. In any case, I am quite sure that the Collection will adequately speak for itself.

*   *   *

Since writing the above in 1963, the collections have grown much larger, but I hope without any diminution of interest or quality. The "judicious pruning" I spoke of above has not yet taken place, and it is a task for the expert which I am happy to leave to more knowledgeable hands. The staff of the Center has my blessing to go about it vigorously, but carefully and thoughtfully, in the future. I am happy to entrust this mature tree and its branches to their tender care.

After the exhibition at the Royal Academy in London in 1964 and the exhibition at Yale in 1965, I thought long and deeply about various alternatives to assure the best ultimate disposition of the corpus of my British collections— not only paintings, but drawings, prints, books and sculptures. Shortly after the Yale exhibition I had a warm and appealing letter from the then Director of the Yale Art Gallery, Andrew Ritchie. I use the word "appealing" advisedly in both its senses; for the letter itself was the acme of *politesse*, while at the same time strongly persuasive as to the advantages of a gift or bequest of the collections to Yale. In preparation for the Yale exhibition, Basil Taylor and I had already had several enjoyable conversations with Andrew, and after receiving his letter I had several more in which he he and I pursued his suggestion further. It was at about this time that Kingman Brewster, as well, assured me of the University's enthusiasm for the idea.

There had always lurked at the back of my mind a tendency to think of my British collecting as the most enjoyable end-product of my Yale and Cambridge education. In addition to exposure to the great Yale teachers— Chauncey Tinker, Fred Pottle, Clyde DeVane, Johnny Berdan, Bob French, Tucker Brooke and many more—I was in later years continually aware of the steady influx of important literary and historical documents to the Yale Library, such as the Boswell and Walpole papers. So that it was natural that I came to associate Yale more and more with the British eighteenth and nineteenth centuries.

While the most advantageous exposure of the works of art was uppermost in my mind (and it would be unrealistic to pretend that our National Gallery of Art in Washington and The Virginia Museum of Fine Arts in Richmond were not, for personal reasons, obvious candidates for large portions of these treasures), it was impossible for me to dismiss this other impelling alternative. Since a university is a community of scholars, a majority of them young scholars at that, and since within its walls there is, or at least should be, a sharing of interests and a cross-fertilization of knowledge, it seemed to me that the ferment of a university would enliven and stimulate the study of and the enjoyment of these artistic relics of our British inheritance, more vitally and more resourcefully than if they were passively displayed in a non-teaching institution.

(However, thanks to the understanding and forbearance of the Director and the Curator of Paintings of the Center, and to their realization that more does not necessarily mean better, it has been possible to lay aside certain paintings for the ultimate benefit of the National Gallery and The Virginia Museum of Fine Arts as well. The Center has also been equally generous in its willingness to forego, at least for the immediate future, the possession of many of the sporting paintings and small intimate landscapes which are such an integral part of two of the houses in which Bunny and I live.)

In 1966 I came to a firm decision, a decision which I confirmed to President Brewster shortly thereafter. I informed him of my intention to give the greatest part of my British collections to Yale, to provide funds to build a suitable building to house them, as well as sufficient endowment to maintain the collections and the building. A part of the endowment funds were further earmarked for the promotion of studies in British art and other British studies, including funds for fellowships, visiting scholars, etc.; but in the meantime soaring building, maintenance and other inflationary costs have proved that our original estimates were somewhat illusory.

In any case, the building and its contents are at last made available permanently for the use and enjoyment of the Yale community, the citizens of New Haven, and the general public of our own country and visitors from abroad. My hope has always been that the Center and its contents would attract undergraduate students, advanced scholars, struggling as well as established artists, and lovers of English art in general—not only for scholastic purposes but for pure enjoyment. It follows that the first responsibility of the Center's staff is the protection and care of the works of art within its walls, and as a corollary, the assiduous upkeep of the building itself. If this responsibility is properly carried out, scholarly use of the treasures within cannot help but flourish, inter-departmental projects cannot help but thrive. While it has always been my hope that the strongest impetus, the central emphasis, would be on the study of British art and artists, it is obvious that there is a wealth of pertinent material waiting for literary scholars, social historians, and those whose researches involve many other disciplines.

After having crossed the Rubicon (or more accurately the Quinnipiac), and I had definitely chosen Yale, my collecting continued unabated, but informed with a slightly different philosophy. With the University, with education, with public exposure in sight, I tried even harder not only to maintain what I considered the high quality of the collections, but wherever possible to add paintings, drawings and books of greater quality and recognized stature. As examples, it was subsequent to my decision to found the Center that I was able to buy such masterpieces as Turner's *Dort*, Reynolds' *Mrs. Abington*, Stubbs' portrait of *Turf*, and his four great shooting paintings now hanging in the Library Court. Other outstanding additions have been the two large Richard Wilsons hanging in the same court, and the Rubens study for the ceiling of the Whitehall Banqueting House. The same held true in respect to the drawing and print collections, to a lesser extent to books. In all of these categories I became more interested, too, in filling in gaps in respect to a general historical survey of British art. The collection, for instance, became better represented by 16th and 17th century artists.

It does not follow that I neglected my own preferences, my personal idiosyncracies of taste, which included a passion for small paintings, representations of the English countryside in watercolors, and scenes of the world of the horse, of hunting and racing. I have to say that I know of several small paintings that I consider the aesthetic equal of my most prestigious large masterpieces, and I reiterate my belief that British sporting art has always, blindly and mistakenly, been grossly underrated.

To sum up. I have tried, as I said in Richmond years ago, to persuade scholars, critics, and the public that British art is multifold, curiously happy, and far more comprehensive than generally realized. And of a special order of excellence.

Those who have helped me have been many, industrious, and wise. Basil Taylor was the earliest, my foremost mentor and friend, and by the time other duties lessened his availability he had instilled in me an ardor for and a vision of British art which has brightened my life ever since.

John Baskett, who on Basil's recommendation came to Virginia from England as my first curator, has continued to be a bulwark of administrative assistance in England, a mine of information, a valued advisor, and a close personal friend.

Dudley Snelgrove, formerly Senior Research Assistant at The British Museum, has been largely responsible for finding, authenticating, recommending and cataloguing most of the drawings and prints bought for the collection from 1970 to the present time. His years of experience in The British Museum, his innate good taste, and his enthusiasm for the pursuit of the rare, the unblemished and the beautiful, will have guaranteed a permanent stamp of excellence on the drawing and print collections.

John Harris, Librarian of the Royal Institute of British Architects, has not only been instrumental in searching for and recommending important architectural and topographical drawings, prints and rare books, but has also found for my approval, and for the improvement of the collections, many desirable paintings and pieces of sculpture. He has also been most helpful in cataloguing a great portion of the collection of architectural drawings.

As to my personal curatorial and bibliographical staff, no praise can be adequately expressed to do justice to the efficiency, untiring energy, and utter indispensability of Beverly Carter, or to the contributions of her assistants, Michelle Tompkins and Alyce Reilly. To Beverly especially I owe heartfelt thanks for her unfailing cheerfulness and humor at times when we have known she has been close to the limit of her endurance. Sincere thanks go to her also for her ability to keep accurate records of everything not only on paper, but in her computer-bank mind as well. Both Yale and I owe her a large debt of gratitude.

Mary Ann Thompson, Librarian of all my British, American, foreign, rare and modern books, also deserves Yale's and my own special thanks. A sudden question about an obscure or presumably missing book has invariably been answered with a cheerful and concise description of its history, peregrinations, and present whereabouts. Quiet, unruffled and unassuming, she has always had the pertinent information at her fingertips.

I am also grateful to Peter Davidock, Registrar of the National Gallery of Art, who has registered, watched over, stored, checked in and out, and personally handled thousands of these works of art which are now at Yale, always with unfailing courtesy and good humor.

Last but certainly not least, I thank Eugene Howard, custodian of all objects whether of art or otherwise at the Brick House, for his faithful, time-consuming and conscientious attention to the physical protection of everything under his care. Whether it is preparing pictures, sculptures, or books for shipment, cleaning and waxing sculptures, oiling and refurbishing books, or repairing or fabricating mounts, slip-cases and solander boxes, he exemplifies the skill of the born craftsman.

Turning from my personal associates and my present staff, I have now to thank those who have represented Yale in the transitional period from the announcement of the intended gift to the final realization of the project. I will always be grateful to Jules Prown and his advisors for their proposal and unqualified endorsement of Louis Kahn as the building's architect. I agreed early in the decision-making stage to that choice, and grew more and more enthusiastic myself as I followed the plans and saw the gradual materialization of the edifice. In the end I look with reverence and pride at the result. But in addition, Jules was a stimulating, affirmative, cooperative colleague and advisor, and it was with real consternation that I learned of his wish to abandon administration and to return to teaching, research, and writing. It has been a loss to the Center and a loss to me personally, but I must congratulate him for his personal integrity and his clarity of purpose.

Turning to the new Director, Ted Pillsbury, and his able staff, I have nothing but confidence and admiration. I now leave the fruits of my amateur husbandry, this sturdy British tree with all its green branches, to him, and to them.

PAUL MELLON
January 1977

William Larkin (active ca. 1609–1619), attributed to

Portrait of an Unknown Man

Oil on panel in a feigned oval
23¾ × 17⅛ in. (59.5 × 43.5 cm.)

A number of elegant full-length portraits from the period 1610–20 have been recently attributed to Larkin, about whom very little is known. His name has been firmly attached to some smaller oval portraits of distinguished sitters, including Lord Herbert of Cherbury. The example reproduced here, together with a companion in an unusual, feigned marble oval, also in the Yale Center for British Art, is of an unknown sitter.

Both are painted with a heightened sense of decorative detail similar to the contemporary miniaturist technique of Isaac Oliver but enlarged to the scale of an easel painting. Unlike other portraits of the late Tudor and early Stuart period, also on view in the Yale Center for British Art, the present picture is less mannered and artificial and gives some insight into the personality of this elegant young man about the court.

TOP LEFT:
Luke Horenbout (fl. 1525–1545),
attributed to
An Unknown Man, aged 35
Bodycolor on card
Circular, 1⅞ in. diameter (4.7 cm.)

TOP RIGHT:
Isaac Oliver (ca. 1556–1617)
Dudley 3rd Lord North
Bodycolor on card
Oval, 2 × 1⅝ in. (5.1 × 4.2 cm.)

CENTER:
Nicholas Hilliard (1547–1619)
A Lady, called Elizabeth, Queen of Bohemia
Bodycolor on card
Oval, 2 × 1⅝ in. (5.1 × 4.2 cm.)

LOWER LEFT:
Samuel Cooper (1609–1672)
A Man called General Fleetwood, 1650
Watercolor on card
Oval, 2½ × 2¼ in. (6.4 × 5.2 cm.)
Signed and dated: 1650

LOWER RIGHT:
Samuel Cooper (1609–1672)
Charles Stuart, 3rd Duke of Richmond
Watercolor on card
Oval, 2¾ × 2¼ in. (7.0 × 5.2 cm.)
Signed with monogram

No survey of art in Great Britain would
be complete without examples of portraits in miniature, of which these are a
representative selection of the early flow-
ering of the "art of limning" now in the
Yale Center for British Art. Elizabethan
miniatures are notable for their jewel-
like detail and brilliant colors, but with
Samuel Cooper a greater realism is
apparent. They represent a period when
portrait miniatures can be said to surpass
native examples of portraiture on the
scale of life.

Claude de Jongh (ca. 1600–1663)

The Thames at Westminster Stairs, 1631

Oil on panel
18¼ × 31½ in. (46.4 × 80 cm.)
Signed and dated lower left:
Aº 163(?1) C d Jongh fecit

The view is taken from a point opposite Westminster Stairs and shows from left to right: the open ground that then marked the edge of London, St. Stephen's Chapel in the Palace of Westminster (destroyed in the fire of 1834), Westminster Hall, the tower of St. Margaret's in front of the Chapter House and Westminster Abbey.

The development of landscape, like portraiture, in seventeenth century England was much improved by the arrival of foreigners. De Jongh, a minor landscape artist, visited England from Holland and brought with him some idea of recent developments there. Instead of a bird's-eye view, de Jongh has painted this London scene in the modern realistic style, with a low viewpoint and feeling for the organization of light and shade in the manner of van Goyen and Esaias van de Velde. The space is layered from a dark foreground, an earthy green middle distance to a dark blue background. The painting depends on two drawings made in 1625, now at Windsor.

3

Sir Anthony Van Dyck (1599–1641)

Portrait of Mountjoy Blount, Earl of Newport

Oil on canvas
85 × 51 in. (215.75 × 129.5 cm.)

After a successful career on the Continent, in Antwerp and Genoa, where he had created a noble style of court portraiture, Van Dyck was invited to England by Charles I in 1632. Here he enjoyed equal success. He revolutionized the prevailing style and produced a series of sensitive and elegant portraits which appealed to and flattered the taste of the King and his court. Van Dyck was knighted and remained in the country, apart from occasional brief visits to the Continent, until his death in 1641.

The Earl of Newport (ca. 1597–1666) was Master of the Ordnance and, in fact, an occasional opponent of Charles I, but he is painted in Van Dyck's best courtly English manner. Against a background of military trappings, the artist has placed his figure, which strides with an exaggerated Baroque swagger. The pose is glamorized by its elongated stature and elegant twist but the idealized figure is individually characterized by Van Dyck's mastery of touch, the delicate colors, the subtle tonality and the sensitive drawing of the face.

William Dobson (1611–1646)

The Streatfeild Family, ca. 1642–43

Oil on canvas
42 × 49½ in. (106.8 × 125.8 cm.)

This portrait probably depicts Richard Streatfeild (born 1611) of Chiddingston, Kent, with his wife Anne and his oldest son Henry (1639–1719). A strip of canvas added sometime after 1647 shows two of his other children, probably William and Alice. Dobson, perhaps the finest English-born painter of the seventeenth century, was employed mainly in Oxford at the court of Charles I during the Civil War. The thickly painted warm facial tones and robust character of this work are typical of his early Oxford paintings.

While influenced by Van Dyck and Venetian painting, this work, with its allegorical background, shows his highly individual style.

Peter Paul Rubens (1577–1640)

Peace Embracing Plenty

Oil on panel
1633–34
24¾ × 18½ in. (62.9 × 47 cm.)

Peter Paul Rubens, the Flemish master whose art and personality dominated Northern European art in the first half of the seventeenth century, visited England in 1629 on a diplomatic mission. While he was there Charles I commissioned him to decorate the ceiling of the Banqueting House in Whitehall, recently completed by Inigo Jones. As in the Marie de' Medici series (now in the Louvre), Rubens created a political allegory glorifying the reign of the first Stuart monarch, James I. In one of the scenes, *The Benefits of the Government of James I,* the present composition occurs emphasizing the amity and abundance enjoyed during the Stuart reign.

The small *modello* is not only for two of the principal figures of the allegory but also, as Julius Held has observed, for the architectural setting behind the figure of King James. Developed studies such as this, executed in gray and brown glazes and touched in local hues (here brilliant gold and a soft rose) on small wooden panels, were submitted to King Charles for approval and became collectors' items in their own right during the artist's lifetime. The brilliance of color, effects of light and robustness of line were especially admired by English artists until the nineteenth century and, significantly, a version of this panel by Rubens formed part of the private art collection of Sir Joshua Reynolds.

Leonard Knyff (1650–1722)

*Black Game, Rabbits and Swallows in the
Park of a Country House*, ca. 1700

Oil on canvas
35½ × 56 in. (90 × 142 cm.)

Knyff came from Holland to London in
1681 and became naturalized in 1694.
Although he was known mostly for his
bird's-eye views of country seats, he also
painted some sporting pictures of game
birds and dogs. In these he followed the
example of Francis Barlow, the earliest
sporting and animal painter to be known
by name. Knyff's landscape, however,
is suffused with a golden light which sets
off his realistic representation of the two
black game cocks displaying their feathers
to the grey hen sitting in the foreground.
The mansion in the background has not
been identified, but a picture like this
would probably have been intended as
part of the decoration, perhaps in the
paneling, of such a country house.

William Hogarth (1697–1764)

The Beggar's Opera, Act III, Scene XI, 1729

Oil on canvas
23¼ × 30 in. (59 × 76 cm.)
Signed: *W^m: Hogarth: Fecit: 1729*

One of several versions by Hogarth of *The Beggar's Opera*, this picture was commissioned by John Rich, manager of the theater in Lincoln's Inn Fields where John Gay's opera opened on January 29, 1728. In the dramatic denouement, the highwayman Macheath faces either execution or the necessity of choosing between his sweetheart and wife who are on their knees appealing to their fathers for mercy. Lavinia Fenton, the actress who played the role of Polly Peachum (at right), later married Charles, 3rd Duke of Bolton, the spectator seated on the far right. The painting is an early example of Hogarth's virtuosity of brushwork as well as an important social commentary on the theater of his day.

William Hogarth (1697–1764)

John Palmer, 1749

Oil on canvas
30 × 25 in. (76.2 × 63.4 cm.)
Signed, bottom left: *W. Hogarth pinxt/
1749*, and inscribed with biographical
details

The sitter was both a barrister of the
Inner Temple and Patron of Ecton,
Northamptonshire, where Hogarth often
stayed. Hogarth's portraiture is at its
best when he is painting someone he
knows well and this lively image has all
the directness of vision and fluid handling
of paint which Hogarth initiated as a
style of English portraiture.

Philip Mercier (ca. 1689–1760)

Sir Edward Hales, Bart., 1744

Oil on canvas
80 × 51 in. (202.5 × 129.5 cm.)
Signed, lower right: *Ph. Mercier Pinxit./anno. 1744*

Mercier was accused by a contemporary of "conceited plaisant [*sic*] Fancies and habits" and certainly, in other examples of his work in the Yale Center for British Art, the influence of Watteau and the French Rococo style is very apparent. In this painting, however, Mercier is much restrained. This sensitive portrait was probably commissioned to celebrate the young man's succession to the baronetcy in 1744 and he is shown as a country squire, with his gun and dog, after a day's shooting. Such a strong sporting emphasis rarely occurs in Mercier's art, although it probably suited the taste of his country patrons.

Joseph Highmore (1692–1780)

The Harlowe Family, ca. 1745–47

Oil on canvas
25½ × 30⅞ in. (64.8 × 78.4 cm.)

Highmore's illustration for Samuel Richardson's *Clarissa* (1747) shows the heroine (standing left) accused by her brother before their parents, uncles, and sister of "having received no less than *five or six visits* at Miss Howe's from the man they had all so much reason to hate. . . ." This is the only surviving painting from an uncompleted set which Highmore had planned to follow his series of twelve paintings of 1744–45 illustrating Richardson's *Pamela*. The lively and responsive poses of the protagonists and the dramatic and complex off-center composition give the scene an immediacy seldom equaled in Highmore's art.

George Beare (active 1740–1750)

*Portrait of an Elderly Lady and a Young
Girl*, 1747

Oil on canvas
50 × 40 in. (127 × 101.5 cm.)
Signed: *Geo. Beare. Pinx/1747*

George Beare, a painter about whom
little is known, was working in
Salisbury in 1747. Around thirty of his
portraits have been traced, most of them
dated in the late 1740s. As represented
in this extraordinarily graphic picture of
youth and old age, his portraits are notable for their unmannered simplicity.
In his directness, expressive brushwork,
and liberal impasto of paint, Beare is a
close provincial counterpart of his contemporary, Hogarth.

Francis Hayman, R.A. (1708–1776)

*Jonathan Tyers with his Daughter
Elizabeth and her Husband John Wood,*
ca. 1750–52

Oil on canvas
39 × 34 in. (99 × 86.3 cm.)

Hayman executed at least seven portraits
of members of the Tyers family, three
of which are in the Yale Center for
British Art. Tyers, proprietor-entrepre-
neur of Vauxhall Gardens and one of
the artist's most important patrons, commissioned Hayman to paint most of the
scenes for the supper-boxes there. They
were perhaps the most publicly visible
paintings in London and exercised a
profound influence.

Arthur Devis (1712–1787)
Mr. and Mrs. Hill, ca. 1748–50
Oil on canvas
30 × 25 in. (76 × 63.5 cm.)

Mr. and Mrs. Hill wait expectantly for five guests for tea. They are posed in the corner of a drawing room by a fireplace ornamented with an Italianate landscape overmantle set into a Rococo plaster-work frame. Arthur Devis devoted virtually his entire forty-year career to small portraiture and conversation pieces, the term describing small scale paintings of real people engaged in everyday informal or domestic activities. With its snapshot quality of arrested motion and meticulous attention to details of costume, possessions, and surroundings, the conversation piece introduced an intimate mood into eighteenth-century British portraiture.

Giovanni Antonio Canal, called
Canaletto (1697–1768)

Old Walton Bridge, 1755

Oil on canvas
18⅛ × 48⅛ in. (46 × 122.2 cm.)

An old inscription on the back by the artist recorded that the painting was commissioned in 1755 by Samuel Dicker, M.P. for Plymouth, whose house is at the extreme left and who had paid for the bridge over the River Thames in 1750. The bridge was constructed of wood with a span of 130 feet and had stone additions at the ends. It was demolished in 1780. The two figures at the right are probably the artist and his patron.

During his stay in London, Canaletto, the famous Venetian view painter, executed about thirty paintings, mostly of the river. These are marked by a clear sense of light and atmosphere. Soon after this work was commissioned, he returned to Italy. The original drawing of the same subject is also in the Yale Center for British Art and another view, seen from a slightly different angle, is in the Dulwich College Gallery.

Samuel Scott (1702/3–1772)

A View over the River Thames towards Westminster, 1749

Oil on canvas
31¼ × 59¼ in. (79.5 × 150.5 cm.)
Signed at bottom left: *S. Scott*

Scott began as a sea painter in the manner of Willem van de Velde and something of that master's luminosity and feeling for sky and water is evident in this painting. Scott turned to London views in emulation of Canaletto who had visited London in 1746. This is a brilliant and interesting example, combining topographical elements with a delicate balance of light and shade.

At the right is the nearly completed Westminster Bridge, finally finished in 1749–50; in the center is Westminster Hall; and at the left is Westminster Abbey with the scaffolding still on one of Hawksmoor's two towers (finished 1744–45). The barge in the foreground bears the arms of the Ironmongers' Company, one of whose members, Sir Samuel Pennent, was elected Lord Mayor of London in 1749. The painting, which includes elements from different dates, probably records a practice run by the barges for the stately procession to Westminster then made by each Lord Mayor every October, an event recorded in a painting by Canaletto also in the collection.

Andrea Soldi (ca. 1703–ca. 1771)

The Sculptor John Michael Rysbrack with his Terra-cotta Statue of Hercules, 1753

Oil on canvas
45 × 35⅞ in. (114.3 × 91.1 cm.)
Signed and dated, lower right:
Aᵈ Soldi Pinxᵗ/Aᵒ 1753

This striking portrait is one of a number of interesting representations of artists and sculptors in the Yale Center for British Art. Rysbrack (1694–1770), Scheemakers and Roubiliac, foreigners like Soldi, were the leaders of their profession in England from early in the 1720s until about 1760, and all are represented in the collection by works of sculpture or in portraits. Soldi came to England from the Levant in about 1738 and he remained until his death, enjoying at first a vogue as a portraitist. He also, incidentally, painted a portrait of Roubiliac (1751, Dulwich Gallery). Rysbrack is shown with calipers in hand dramatically pointing to the terra cotta model of his marble statue of Hercules executed for the Pantheon at Stourhead. A model for the head is in the collection. Horace Walpole described the figure as "an exquisite summary of his skill, knowledge and judgement," which Soldi has emphasized in a lively fashion.

Allan Ramsay (1713–1784)

Mary (Robertson), Mrs. William Adam (1699–1761), 1754

Oil on canvas
37 × 28 in. (94 × 71 cm.)
Signed: *A. Ramsay/1754*

Mary Robertson married William Adam in 1716 and the architects, Robert (born 1728) and James (born 1732), were her third and fourth sons. Ramsay was a friend of the family and especially sensitive to Scottish character. Mrs. Adam was a severe critic of her sons' social extravagance.

The portrait, painted at a time when there was increasing competition between Ramsay and Reynolds, is an outstanding example of Ramsay's contribution to the natural tradition of British portraiture.

John Hamilton Mortimer, A.R.A.
(1740–1779)

Sergeant-at-Arms Bonfoy, his Son (?) and John Clementson, Snr., ca. early 1770s

Oil on canvas
40 × 50 in. (101.5 × 127 cm.)

The bold modeling of forms, restrained style, and solid characterization of the sitters in this impressive conversation piece are typical of Mortimer's portraits from the early 1770s. The young man at the left, thought perhaps to be Bonfoy's son, was painted out from 1903 (and probably earlier) until the work was sold at auction in 1959. Bonfoy (seated at the left) was Sergeant-at-Arms from 1752 until his death in 1775, and John Clementson served as Deputy Sergeant-at-Arms from 1770 to 1804. Check-patterned furniture frequently recurs in Mortimer's portraits. The views of London Bridge by Herbert Pugh, seen on the back wall in the portrait, were exhibited (or versions of them) at the Society of Arts in 1767 and are now in the Bank of England, London.

Charles Brooking (1723–1759)

English Shipping in a Breeze in the Channel

Oil on canvas
35½ × 46⅜ in. (90 × 118 cm.)
Signed bottom left center on a spar of
wood: *C. Brooking*

The ship in the foreground is probably an Indiaman who has just dropped the pilot in the small lugger. At the left is a two-decker naval ship running before the wind under easy sail. At the right is a frigate under sail, with a flagship and other vessels in the background. The scene takes place on the Downs near the North and South Foreland. Its eighteenth century title was *Evening*, a suitable title for a picture whose timelessness and poise transcends the mere accuracy of Brooking's realism. Little in detail is

known of Brooking who specialized in marine subjects, but he was the most atmospheric of the English followers of the van de Veldes.

Dominic Serres, R.A. (1722–1793)

An English Two-Decker Lying Hove to with Other Ships and Vessels in a Fresh Breeze, 1770

Oil on panel
15¾ × 25 in. (40 × 135 cm.)
Signed and dated on a spar at right:
D. Serres 1770

Serres was a French seaman who was captured by the English and then began his career as an artist. He even became a founding member of the Royal Academy in 1769.

Of the generation of marine painters after Brooking, he successfully exploited the complications of composition and boisterous sense of atmosphere and choppy sea which led the way to the all-enveloping sea paintings of Turner. Here a naval two-decker which bears a commodore's pennant at the main top masthead is hove to with a cutter running under her stern, perhaps delivering something to the frigate close hauled at the right.

Richard Wilson, R.A. (1714–1782)

A View of Rome from the Villa Madama,
1753

Oil on canvas
38 × 52 in. (96.5 × 132 cm.)
Signed in monogram, lower center:
RW/1753

Wilson turned to landscape painting during his stay in Italy from 1750–57. He developed a style of ideal landscape painting which owed much to Claude and which, in turn, influenced a whole generation of landscape painters, particularly the young Turner. This is one of his finest Italian scenes, and was actually painted in Rome. Many of his other Italian views were painted after his return to England in 1757, and by repetition often decline in quality. This, however, is subtly organized with a cool light breaking over the magical distances and view of Rome, as seen from the heights of the terraces of the Villa Madama.

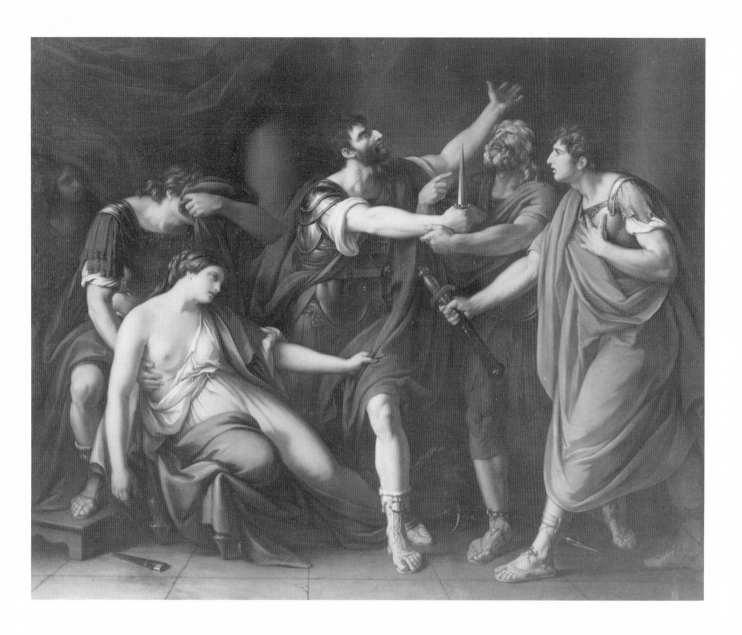

Gavin Hamilton (1723–1798)

The Oath of Brutus, ca. 1763–64

Oil on canvas
84 × 104 in. (213.3 × 264 cm.)

This is most likely the original painting commissioned from Hamilton by James Hope (later 3rd Earl of Hopetoun) and engraved by Domenico Cunego in 1768. There are at least three other recorded versions, one of which is at the Drury Lane Theatre, London. The subject is taken from Livy, Book I, 59, 1–2, and depicts the moment when Valerius and Lucretius join Brutus in an oath against Tarquinius to avenge the rape and suicide of Lucretia. The shallow stagelike space, heroic forms, simplicity and severity of Hamilton's style underscore the solemnity of the theme. The compositional format that he established for the oath motif was to have a great impact on the Continent in the decades that followed.

Johann Zoffany, R.A. (1734/5–1810)

The Drummond Family, ca. 1769

Oil on canvas
41½ × 63 in. (104 × 160 cm.)

In this, one of Zoffany's most charming conversation pieces, are represented three generations of the Drummond family. Andrew Drummond (1688–1769), the founder of Drummond's Bank, is seated in the center. This figure, which may be posthumous, is taken from an earlier single portrait by Zoffany. Andrew's son John Drummond, M.P., is at the left, between the latter's younger son John (born 1766), who is supported by a groom, and his daughter Jane on the grey pony. At the right, is Andrew Drummond's daughter-in-law Charlotte and two other grandchildren, Charlotte and George. The whole presents a de-lightfully informal gathering in a rural setting at Stanmore Middlesex, with a distant view of Harrow-on-the-Hill.

George Stubbs, A.R.A. (1724–1806)

Two Gentlemen Out Shooting, III, 1769

Oil on canvas
40 × 50 in. (101.6 × 127 cm.)

This is one of a series of four in the Yale Center for British Art devoted to shooting scenes which Stubbs exhibited between 1767 and 1770. They were later engraved with trite verses attached which gave the sequence of the shooting expedition, though as Stubbs exhibited them separately, it is not entirely clear what his real meaning was. They remain, however, as marvelous examples of his landscape painting, with that balance, subtlety of light and shade and harmony of tone for which he is unsurpassed, but also, perhaps, with more anecdotal action than he normally allows himself.

George Stubbs, A.R.A. (1724–1806)

Two Cream Ponies, a Phaeton and a Stable Lad, ca. 1780–85

Oil on panel
35 × 53½ in. (89 × 136 cm.)

This late work probably dates from the 1780s, perhaps from before 1785. Ponies of this cream color were sufficiently rare for them to be made a subject in themselves but, as in all his paintings of horses, accuracy of anatomy and a tame delineation of a given spot were not enough. There is an exquisite sense of poise and arrangement, a refined sense of color, a subtle balance of light and shade, with the principal forms carefully placed against the poetic landscape in the background.

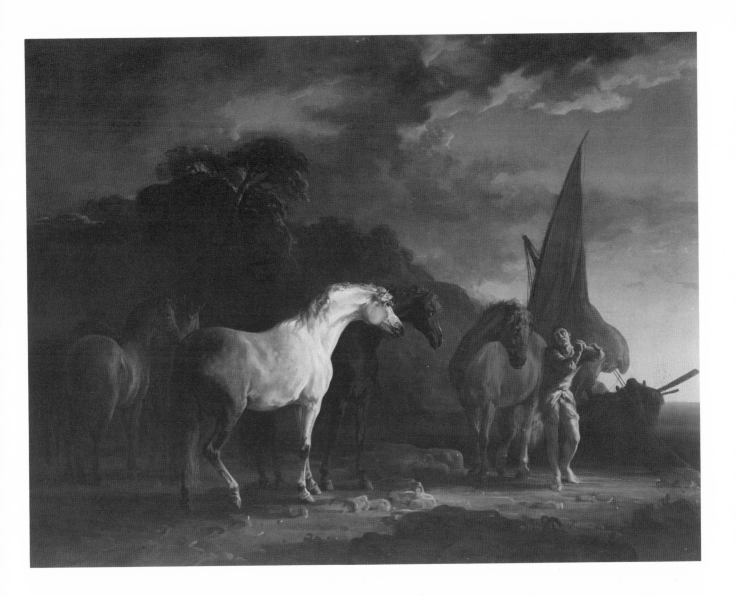

Sawrey Gilpin, R.A. (1733–1807)

Gulliver Taking his Final Leave of his Master, the Sorrel Nag, and the Land of the Houyhnhnms, ca. 1771

Oil on canvas
41 × 55 in. (104.2 × 139.7 cm.)
Signed lower left: *S Gilpin*

Between 1768 and 1772, Gilpin exhibited three scenes from Swift's *Gulliver's Travels* at the Society of Arts. In addition to this work, a version of which is in the Whitbread Collection, Southill, he painted *Gulliver Addressing the Houyhnhnms Supposing Them to be Conjurors* (versions are in the Yale Center for British Art and the Ministry of Works, London) and *Gulliver Reprimanded and Silenced by his Master, When Describing the Horrors of War* (City of York Art Gallery). Although mainly an animal painter, Gilpin introduced an imaginative approach to the genre by frequently choosing historical or literary themes which featured horses among the principal figures. This, of course, made his works more acceptable at the Academy.

Thomas Gainsborough, R.A. (1727–1788)

William Lowndes, 1771

Oil on canvas
50 × 40 in. (127 × 116 cm.)

With a ravishing display of paint, Gainsborough shows that he could on occasions rival Reynolds in portraying old men of character. As the inscription records, Lowndes was in his eighty-fourth year when the portrait was painted, and something of the old man's fright at sitting for his portrait, particularly so late in life, is conveyed in his expression. He was an auditor of the exchequer, possibly another reason for his tight-lipped look.

Thomas Gainsborough, R.A. (1727–1788)

A Coastal Landscape with a Shepherd and his Flock, ca. 1785

Oil on canvas
25 × 30 in. (63.5 × 76 cm.)

At the end of his career, Gainsborough was not only concerned with creating a personal landscape vision of timeless Arcadian mood, but he also experimented with ephemeral light effects, so that some of his landscape paintings look like drawings and some of his oils look like pastels. He even painted colored transparencies on glass, lit from behind with a flickering light. The movement of light and the coloring of the two landscapes reproduced here give some idea of the variety within his late romantic style. This work dates from the mid-1780s.

Thomas Gainsborough, R.A. (1727–1788)

A Mountain Valley with Figures and Sheep, ca. 1786–88

Oil on canvas
48 × 58¾ in. (122 × 149 cm.)

Gainsborough's late landscapes are much removed in spirit from the early "Dutch landskips" he remembered with so much affection. A quiet fresh naturalism has been replaced by a more personal approach to nature, to some extent in conscious imitation of Gaspard Poussin. Gainsborough no longer recorded what he saw but rather painted an idea of landscape. The mountains, valleys, shepherds and woods were often suggested by rocks, twigs and grasses which he arranged on his painting table for compositional effect. This romantic vision is one of a number of mountainous views he produced at the end of his life, ca. 1786.

Sir Joshua Reynolds, P.R.A. (1723–1792)

Miss Sarah Campbell, ca. 1777–78

Oil on canvas
49 × 39 in. (124.3 × 99 cm.)

During the 1770s Reynolds' portraiture
had developed a new amplitude and confidence of pose. This fine example, which
was paid for in January 1778, shows well
his dominant role as a portrait painter,
with the subtle twist of the figure, perhaps based on classical models, and the
brilliance of the handling. The sitter,
Miss Sarah Campbell, was the sister of
John, 1st Lord Cawdor, also painted by
Reynolds. She married a barrister,
Thomas Wodehouse, in 1782.

Sir Joshua Reynolds, P.R.A. (1723–1792)

Charles Stanhope, 3rd Earl of Harrington, 1782

Oil on canvas
93 × 56 in. (236.25 × 143.5 cm.)
Annotated in contemporary hand, lower left: *Charles Earl of Harrington;* and lower right: *S.r J. Reynolds. Pinx.t*

Exhibited at the Royal Academy in 1783 (no. 193), this portrait is a fine example of the grand style which Reynolds and his contemporaries so much admired. Lord Harrington (1756–1829), accompanied by a black page, is heroically posed in a manner recalling the *Apollo Belvedere.* The warring forces in the background allude to his distinguished career as a soldier, having served as Aide-de-Camp to General Burgoyne in the American War of Independence in 1777 and as a commander in Jamaica in 1780. Reynolds' account books record numerous sittings during 1782. Reynolds also painted several portraits of Lord Harrington's wife Jane both before and after their marriage in 1779, one of which with her sons, Charles and Lincoln, ca. 1786–92 is in the collection of the Yale University Art Gallery.

Joseph Wright of Derby, A.R.A.
(1743–1797)

The Blacksmith's Shop, 1771

Oil on canvas
50½ × 41 in. (128.3 × 104 cm.)
Signed and dated: *Joş Wright/Pinxʲ 1771*

Wright described the creation of this
majestic modern scene as "Two men
forming a bar of iron into a horseshoe
from whence the light must proceed.
An idle fellow may stand by the anvil
in a time-killing posture. . . . Horse shoes
hanging upon ye walls. . . ." In another
room "a farrier may be shoeing a horse
by the light of a candle. . . . This will be
an indication of an accident having
happened. . . . The moon may appear. . . ."
   Out of this collection of everyday
anecdotal details, Wright has created a
carefully posed masterpiece of light
effects, imbued with a sense of heroic
grandeur in the tradition of Le Nain
(*Vulcan's Forge*) or Georges de la Tour.
Paintings of contemporary life painted
with subtle light effects became one of
Wright's specialties.

Joseph Wright of Derby, A.R.A.
(1734–1797)

The Rev. and Mrs. Thomas Gisborne, 1786

Oil on canvas
73 × 60 in. (185.5 × 152.5 cm.)
Signed and dated: *J. Wright pinx! 1786*

Wright himself called this double portrait a "conversation picture" and he is
at some pains to emphasize in an informal
way the sitter's accomplishments. The
Rev. Thomas Gisborne (1758–1846)
came from a distinguished family in
Derby, and Wright had painted his portrait when Gisborne was an undergraduate in Cambridge in 1777. He went on
to become a well-known author on
moral philosophy, an active philanthropist, a curate of Barton-under-Need-
wood, Staffordshire, a prebendary of
Durham Cathedral and a friend of the
artist. His intellectual pursuits were an
important influence on Wright who has
shown him with his sketching equipment, contemplating nature in the company of his wife, the former Miss Mary
Babington, whom he had married three
years earlier.

Pompeo Girolamo Batoni (1708–1789)

Portrait of a Lady, called Lady Hippisley, 1785

Oil on canvas
29½ × 25 in. (75 × 63.5 cm.)
Signed: *Pompeo. De./Batoni. Pinx./Romae. 1785*

For the Englishman traveling on the Grand Tour, Batoni was the most sought-after portrait painter in Rome. His long and eminent career, beginning in the 1740s, involved a wide patronage and was financially rewarding. In 1778, James Northcote wrote that, after painting the portrait of a cardinal, Batoni rejected the offer of a "diamond cross to wear at the bosom of his coat . . . and said he had a drawerful at home." The painting is one of Batoni's latest known works, exemplifying the exquisite drafts-manship and bold treatment of pose which appealed to his British audience. In this particular example, the identity of the sitter is not known, and this deli-cate image may be of someone close to Batoni's circle, since Lady Hippisley and her husband were not in Rome in 1785.

Joseph Mallord William Turner, R.A.
(1775–1851)

Harlech Castle, 1799

Oil on canvas
34½ × 47 in. (87 × 119.5 cm.)

The view of the castle is based on sketches Turner made on a tour of Wales in 1798. It was exhibited at the Royal Academy in 1799 with lines from Milton's *Paradise Lost*:

> Now came still evening on and twi-
> light grey
> Had in her sober livery all things clad.
> . . . Hesperus that led
> The starry host rode brightest till the
> moon
> Rising in clouded majesty unveiled
> her peerless light.

A contemporary critic rightly noted that "this landscape, though it combines the style of Claude and of our excellent Wilson, yet wears an aspect of originality that shows the Painter looks at Nature with his own eyes." It marks the beginning of a series of confrontations which Turner made between his art and the art of the past and of his recent contemporaries.

Joseph Mallord William Turner, R.A.
(1775–1851)

*Dort or Dordrecht, the Dort Packet-Boat
from Rotterdam Becalmed*, 1818

Oil on canvas
62 × 92 in. (157.5 × 233 cm.)
Signed: *J.M.W. Turner, R.A., 1818 Dort*

This famous masterpiece was painted after Turner had made his first trip to Holland and Germany in 1817 and shows a packet boat becalmed, with the Grote Kerk of Dordrecht in the distance. It was exhibited at the Royal Academy in 1818 and bought from there by Turner's great friend and patron, Walter Fawkes, in whose family it remained until quite recently. With its great sense of detail and its scale, suffused by an all-enveloping light, the painting marks a climax in Turner's career. On the one hand it can be seen as a culmination of his study of old masters, with its obvious debt to Cuyp in style and subject matter, and on the other hand, it looks forward, in its subtlety and brilliance of lighting, to his personal visions of the latter part of his career.

John Constable, R.A. (1776–1837)

Dedham Vale with Ploughman, ca. 1814

Oil on canvas
16¾ × 30 in. (42.5 × 76 cm.)

In 1814 Constable wrote to John Dunthorne, Sr., an early friend, probably about this picture, that he had added "some ploughman to the landscape from the park pales which is a great help, but I must try and warm the picture a little more if I can. But it will be difficult as 'tis now all of a piece—it is bleak and looks as if there would be a shower of sleet, and that you know is too much the case with my things." The painting was later engraved in mezzotint by David Lucas and given the title *A Summerland*, which does not refer to the season but rather to the plowing of land which had been left fallow the previous year, a common local practice around Constable's home in East Bergholt. By such accurate observation Constable laid the basis for his larger romantic visions.

John Constable, R.A. (1776–1837)

Hadleigh Castle, the Mouth of the Thames —Morning, after a Stormy Night, 1829

Oil on canvas
48 × 64¾ in. (122 × 164.5 cm.)

This romantic image was based on sketches made fifteen years previously on a visit to Southend where Constable was impressed by the "melancholy grandeur of the sea shore" and the views from the castle ruin of the Kent hills, the Nore and North Foreland. The painting, for which he also produced a full-size sketch (now in the Tate Gallery, London) was exhibited at the Royal Academy in 1829, with a quotation from Thomson's *Summer*:

> The desert joys
> Wildly, though all his melancholy bounds

Rude ruins glitter; and the briny deep,
Seen from some pointed promontory's top,
Far to the dim horizon's utmost verge
Restless, reflects a floating gleam.

Although the powerful emotional appeal of the picture may have had something to do with Constable's sadness at the recent death of his wife, the painting can also be seen as a development of his interest in the "bolder phenomena of nature," with its variety of atmospheric effects and its forceful play of light and dark.

George H. Harlow (1787–1819)

Henry Fuseli, 1817

Oil on panel
21 × 16⅛ in. (53.3 × 41 cm.)

Henry Fuseli, R.A. (1741–1825) was Professor of Painting and Keeper at the Royal Academy. His own work was devoted mainly to historical painting of obscure and nightmarish visions, but many anecdotes survive which testify to his kindness as a teacher and liveliness as a personality. Nollekens, their contemporary, recounts how Fuseli gave Harlow "every possible advantage, by affording him numerous sittings" for what turned out to be "one of the most dignified and characteristic likenesses of Fuseli." The painting was exhibited at the Academy in 1817.

Sir Thomas Lawrence, P.R.A. (1769–1830)

George James Welbore Agar-Ellis, ca. 1825

Oil on canvas
36 × 29 in. (91.5 × 73.75 cm.)

Towards the end of his life, Lawrence produced some of his most sparkling portraits. This fine example represents a contemporary politician and generous patron of the arts, George James Welbore Agar-Ellis, later 1st Lord Dover (1797–1833) and was painted ca. 1825. Agar-Ellis was described by Macaulay as a "nobleman of amiable manners, of untarnished public and private character and of cultivated mind." He acted as one of the pall bearers at the artist's funeral in 1830.

Francis Danby, A.R.A. (1793–1861)

Children by a Brook, ca. 1820–22

Oil on panel
29½ × 24½ in. (74.9 × 62.2 cm.)
Signed bottom left: *F. Danby*

Danby's varied artistic career which began in Ireland, took him to Dublin and
London before he settled in Bristol where
he lived between 1813 and 1822. This
picture was probably painted at the end
of this period. He became best known
for his large scale dramatic paintings,
similar to those of John Martin, which
he painted before he left for Switzerland
in 1829.

   His early Bristol work, such as this
and another, *A View of Avon Gorge*, in
the Yale Center for British Art, are
gentle romantic images, influenced by
William Collins whose work *The Young
Anglers* was exhibited at the Royal
Academy in 1814. The scene shows
children with a toy boat, probably on
the River Frome near Stapleton. The
delicate play of light and shade and the
absorption of the participants very much
accords with the sentiment of a friend
of his who remarked, "There is nothing
but poetry about the existence of
childhood."

Richard Parkes Bonington (1802–1828)

A Fish Market, Boulogne, ca. 1824

Oil on canvas
32 × 48 in. (81.3 × 122 cm.)

The Yale Center for British Art is particularly rich in works by Bonington of which this is, perhaps, the finest. Bonington's upbringing as an artist was in France, but through the tuition of Francia, he acquired knowledge of the English watercolor tradition which can be seen in the fluid handling of this large oil. He painted a number of beach scenes after a visit to northern France in 1823. This glowing example, with a subtle arrangement of planes and tones and an ambitious effect of light directed at the spectator, is handled with that precision of touch which Delacroix so much admired.

John Martin (1789–1854)

The Bard

Oil on canvas
50 × 40 in. (127 × 101.5 cm.)

Martin made his reputation by painting a series of large scale epic pictures which contain much romantic theatricality. The subject, painted in Martin's most flamboyant epic manner, is taken from Thomas Gray's ode, *The Bard*. It commemorates the Welsh tradition that Edward I, after he had completed the conquest of Wales, ordered that all the bards who fell into his hands be put to death:

> Robed in the sable garb of woe,
> With haggard eyes the Poet stood;
> (Loose his beard, and hoary hair
> Streamed, like a meteor, to the troubled air)

Martin exhibited a larger version at the Royal Academy in 1817 which is now in the Laing Art Gallery, Newcastle-upon-Tyne.

William Blake (1757–1827)

Virgin and Child, 1825

Tempera and oil, heightened with gold
11¼ × 9¼ in. (28.5 × 23.5 cm.)
Signed lower right: *Freso* [sic]/*1825*/*Blake*

Blake painted a series of religious and
allegorical paintings between 1790 and
1825 in a mixed medium which he described as "tempera." The technique,
however, bore little relation to true
tempera painting and Blake's experi-
ments account for the damaged quality
of the painting. The image, however,
remains as a very personal interpretation
of a conventional theme suggesting over-
tones of Indian art in the representation
of the Virgin.

Samuel Palmer (1805–1881)

The Harvest Moon, ca. 1833

Oil on panel
8¾ × 10⅞ in. (21.9 × 27.8 cm.)
Signed lower left: *S. PALMER*

Palmer's best known works are from the period which began in 1824 and lasted until the early 1830s when, inspired by William Blake and the pastoral setting in and around the village of Shoreham in Kent, he created landscapes of visionary intensity. *The Harvest Moon*, which comes from the collection of the artist's son, A. H. Palmer, dates from the late Shoreham period and is almost certainly the same work exhibited at the Royal Academy in 1833. The harvesters, laboring peacefully beneath a full moon, are in harmony with an abundant nature. Although less intensely personal, this painting still captures much of the poetic mood of the earlier Shoreham works.

Joseph Stannard (1797–1830)

Buckenham Ferry, 1826

Oil on panel
15¾ × 24 in. (40 × 61 cm.)
Signed and dated: *J. Stannard 1826*

A group of young artists around John Crome began exhibiting together in Norwich and they became known as the Norwich School. Buckenham Ferry is on the River Yare midway between Yarmouth and Stannard's native Norwich. He had visited Holland in 1821 and this painting reveals something of the clarity of light and simple realism which he, among others of the Norwich School, had learned from the Dutch.

James Collinson (1825–1881)

A Mother on a Stile with her Daughter,
Culver Cliff, Isle of Wight, in the Distance

Oil on panel
20¾ × 16⅝ in. (52.5 × 42 cm.)

The Pre-Raphaelites astounded the public by their early belief in truth to nature, as opposed to what they regarded as the generalized sloppiness of their predecessors. The result, in their landscapes, was a bright, high-keyed palette and insistent detail as if they saw "nature without eyelids," which was not always without a certain deliberate awkwardness of pose and composition. Collinson, a founding but not very successful member of the Pre-Raphaelite Brotherhood, visited the Isle of Wight in 1849 with William Michael Rossetti, the group's chronicler, while Collinson was engaged to Christina Rossetti.

John Frederick Herring, Snr. (1795–1865)

Harvest, 1857

Oil on canvas
41 ¹³/₁₆ × 73 ³/₁₆ in. (106.2 × 183.3 cm.)
Signed and dated: *J.F. Herring Sen. 1857*

Although Herring is best known for his paintings of horses and hunting pictures, in this impressive work he has extended his range to include a panoramic landscape and anecdotal detail. The bright coloring and insistent realism may owe something to the influence of the Pre-Raphaelites whose work had become well known in the 1850s.

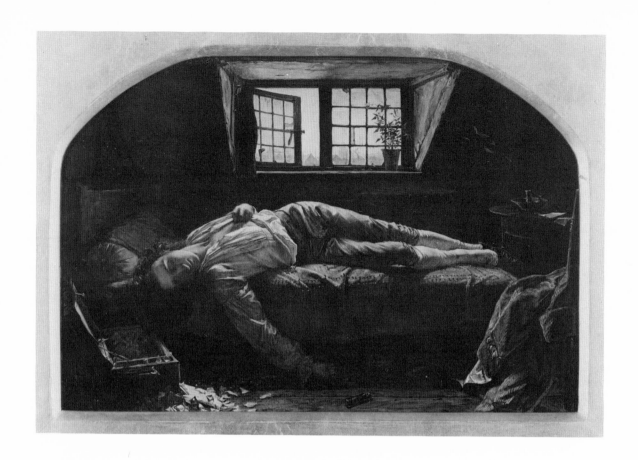

Henry Wallis, R.W.S. (1830–1916)

The Death of Chatterton

Oil on panel
8 15/16 × 11 7/8 in. (22.7 × 30.2 cm.) arched top
Signed: *H. Wallis*

Wallis combined the poetic and romantic aspects of Pre-Raphaelitism with the sentimental approach of Victorian art in this well-known painting of the suicide of the poet Chatterton, whose poems lie destroyed on the floor together with the fatal phial. This is a smaller version of the work which Wallis exhibited at the Royal Academy in 1856 with the lines:

> Cut is the branch that might have
>   grown full straight,
> And burned is Apollo's laurel bough.

Francis Barlow (1626?–1704)

Man Hunting with a Staff and Hound,
ca. 1660

Pen and brown ink
4¾ × 6 in. (122 × 153 mm.)
Inscribed, lower right: *Frañ Barlow/*
invent it
T. E. Lowinsky Collection

Often referred to as the "father of British sporting art," Francis Barlow was the first native artist to specialize in animal subjects. His work is known today principally through the many etchings and engravings that he and others made after his designs. This pen and ink sketch of a man and dog could be a study for a hunting scene to be painted or engraved. The wiry lines and careful hatching technique suggest that the drawing was executed early in Barlow's career, when his style was much influenced by the study of engravings. The elaborate signature in the lower right corner is similar to inscriptions on prints, which were usually signed with the artist's name and the Latin word *invenit* or *delineavit* ("invented" or "drew" it). Perhaps this sketch is for a stag hunt, for the broadsword which the man wears is shown in a Barlow print of that subject, and the dog is of the same breed usually released to kill the stag after it had been run down by lighter coursing dogs. It has also been suggested that the sport depicted is otter hunting.

William Hogarth (1697–1764)

Drawing for Plate I of
The Four Stages of Cruelty, ca. 1750

Pencil and red chalk, indented for transfer
15½ × 13¼ in. (393 × 335 mm.)

Hogarth's fame as an artist derives as
much from his many series of popular
satirical prints as from his paintings. This
is a drawing for Plate I of *The Four Stages
of Cruelty*, four engravings published in
1751 which sold for one shilling each.
The series traces the career of Tom Nero,
the young ruffian in the center of this
scene, through his early assaults on animals to his days as a brutal carriage driver
and highwayman and eventually to his
conviction as a murderer whose corpse,
as a just reward of cruelty, is used for
dissection in a medical school. The pre-
paratory drawing shows Hogarth's
characteristic nervous, active line which
will become firm and definite when
transferred to the copper plate; the
placing of figures was closely followed in
the finished engraving, although in reverse. Hogarth hoped to reach the wid-
est possible audience with these prints,
and the verses by the Reverend James
Townley at the bottom of the engraving
convey the moralizing intention of the
artist:

> Learn from this fair Example—You
>   Whom savage Sports delight,
> How Cruelty disgusts the view
>   While Pity charms the sight.

William Taverner (1703–1772)

Landscape with Nymphs Bathing, ? ca. 1750

Watercolor and bodycolor
12½ × 15½ in. (318 × 395 mm.)
Inscribed on verso: *Nymphs Bathing Polinburg*

Although he was not a professional artist, William Taverner devoted much of his time to painting and drawing landscape. His compositions rarely represent any specific site, but his technique is typical of topographical "stained" drawings, that is, thin washes of watercolor over a monochrome underpainting. Inspired by the Italianate precedents of Claude and Poussin, he often produced classical scenes populated with mythological figures which were much admired by his contemporaries. In this example, the artist employs delicate effects of light and atmosphere to create an idealized stage for the bathing nymphs. The inscription on the back of the drawing suggests that the composition is adapted from one of the paintings of the Italianate Dutch artist, Cornelius von Poelenburg (1586–1667).

Richard Wilson, R.A. (1714–1782)

Shepherd Seated under a Tree, ca. 1755

Black and white chalk on grey paper
15¾ × 10 in. (402 × 252 mm.)

Although he was trained as a portrait
painter, Richard Wilson's real talent was
for landscape. While in Italy between
1750 and 1756, he was encouraged to
devote himself to landscape painting by
Francesco Zuccarelli and Claude-Joseph
Vernet. He soon developed an original
style, firmly based on detailed observation of the natural scene, especially in the
Roman campagna. Here he executed
many drawings on the spot, including
probably this careful study of two trees,
where, by the delicate modulation of
chalk, he successfully conveys the details
of foliage, light and shade. By adding
the little figure of the shepherd, Wilson
gives the scene a pastoral touch and a
new sense of scale. The drawing is no
longer a mere study after nature: it is on
its way to becoming a classical composition.

Paul Sandby, R.A. (1730–1809)

Imaginary Landscape with a Group of Trees and Distant Town, ca. 1760

Pen and grey ink, pencil and watercolor
Sight: 14½ × 21 in. (370 × 533 mm.)
Thomas Girtin Collection

Although he was trained in the highly disciplined topographical tradition, Paul Sandby approached landscape with extremely fresh and varied style and technique. As one of the first artists to make sketching tours throughout Britain, he was an important influence on Girtin, Turner and Cotman. His technical advances included improvements in the aquatint process and the popularization of the opaque medium of bodycolor. Even more significant was his role in raising the status of watercolor drawings, which he exhibited publicly from 1760 to the end of his life. This imaginary landscape shows the influence of French rococo art with its delicate, graceful rhythms. Sandby first attracts the viewer's eye with the beautifully drawn group of trees; then, the gently receding road leads to the distant town and mountains deep in the background.

Joseph Wright of Derby, A.R.A.
(1734–1797)

Self-Portrait, ca. 1768

White and black chalk
14¼ × 10⅞ in. (360 × 278 mm.)

Even in the field of portraiture, Joseph
Wright allowed the phenomena of light
to play an important role. This drawing,
which may be a self-portrait, is strongly
lit from the left, creating dramatic contrasts of light and shadow. Stylistically,
Wright's drawing is extremely close to
the mezzotints and chalk drawings executed in about 1760 by Thomas Frye
(1710–1762): large scale heads in which
soft and luminous highlights play against
velvety shadows. It may well be that
Frye's work suggested the form to
Wright.

William Pars, A.R.A. (1742–1782)

*The Secundini Monument at Ighel in the
Duchy of Luxembourg*, ca. 1775

Watercolor with pen and grey ink and
some bodycolor
13¼ × 20 in. (334 × 507 mm.)

William Pars was one of a number of
eighteenth century artists who traveled
as professional draftsmen in the company
of noblemen on the Grand Tour or on
antiquarian expeditions. He was sent by
the Dilettante Society with an expedition to Asia Minor and Greece in 1764–
66; and in 1770, with Viscount Palmer-
ston, he visited Switzerland, northern
Italy, the Rhine region, and Luxembourg. The first version of the watercolor shown here was drawn for Palmer-
ston's own collection and appeared at
the Royal Academy in 1771. Later Pars
made two more drawings of the same
scene; this one was probably executed
in 1775 just before he left for Rome,

where he died from pneumonia, con-
tracted while drawing in the water at
Tivoli. His gentle use of color and sensitive response to both landscape and
architecture can be seen in this work.
The Secundini Monument is now preserved in the Landesmuseum at Trier.

John Robert Cozens (1752–1797)

The Aiguille Verte, ca. 1778

Pen and black ink, grey and brown
wash over pencil
9⅜ × 14⅛ in. (240 × 360 mm.)

Despite his short career, John Robert Cozens was one of the most influential watercolorists in eighteenth century England. His early training came from his father, Alexander Cozens, but he developed his own poetic style of handling the medium. Both Turner and Girtin copied his work when they attended the evening drawing classes held by Dr. Monro at his home in the Adelphi. Constable regarded him as "the greatest genius that ever touched landscape." Cozens made two trips to Italy (1776–79 and 1782–83), and returned with a store of drawings which were to serve him as subjects for watercolor commissions for the next nine years. During his first trip abroad, Cozens drew this view of a mountain peak in Switzerland for Richard Payne Knight, the connoisseur and benefactor of the British Museum. It is typical of the drawings he executed which were later expanded into impressive, atmospheric mountain landscapes. A large version of this subject is in an English private collection. Unfortunately, by 1794 Cozens had become incurably insane and was no longer able to work.

John Hamilton Mortimer, A.R.A.
(1740–1779)

Choir and Orchestra, ca. 1779

Pen and black ink
8⅛ × 11⅛ in. (208 × 282 mm.)

John Hamilton Mortimer was a prodigy in drawing and the envy of his fellow students in London. When he was only twenty-three, he won first prize for a historical painting from the Society of Artists. His work has astonishing variety and includes conversation pieces, history paintings, self-portraits, book illustrations, satire, imaginary banditti, and monsters. The drawing here is a satire on European national types; the musicians are labeled, from left to right: English, Swiss, Italian, German, and Prussian. The singers crowded above present a mélange of different ages and physiognomies. Skillfully drawn and shaded with stippling similar to that in Mortimer's etched work, the composition is derived from a formula established by Hogarth in his satires, such as *A Chorus of Singers* of 1732 and *The Laughing Audience* of about 1733. A replica of *Choir and Orchestra* is in the Queen's Collection; and the subject was etched by Lydia Bates.

John Raphael Smith (1752–1812)

A Woman Tending a Carnation Plant,
ca. 1775

Black, red and white chalk
12⅝ × 9½ in. (320 × 242 mm.)

This charming chalk drawing illustrates
a kind of casual portraiture of English
society for which J. R. Smith was well
known. Essentially self-taught, Smith
became a skillful mezzotint engraver;
his early success was based on his popular
mezzotint copies of paintings by Reynolds, Romney and others. In their years
of apprenticeship, both Turner and Girtin were employed by Smith to hand-
color his prints. Later, in 1802, Peter De
Wint became Smith's pupil for a short
time. Although mezzotint was Smith's
forte, he also worked in chalk and in oil,
and he exhibited in both these media at
the Royal Academy. A modern inscription on the back of the drawing, considered erroneous, identifies the young
woman as Princess Amelia, daughter of
George II.

Thomas Gainsborough, R.A.
(1727–1788)

Wooded Landscape, ca. 1780

Black and white chalk on blue paper
11¼ × 16 in. (286 × 408 mm.)

Gainsborough drew for many purposes, but primarily for recreation. Sketching was a release from the pressures of his fashionable portrait practice, an avenue of escape through which he could freely express his delight in natural scenes. His landscapes, in oil and other media, rarely represent an actual place; instead, they are generalized and imaginary, evocations of pastoral tranquility and the fashionable Theory of the Picturesque. The figures in them, as he himself wrote, serve as accents, to "fill a place (I won't say stop a Gap) to create a little business for the Eye to be drawn from the Trees in order to return to them with more glee." In this drawing, Gainsborough employs Italian chalk—a medium he used frequently in the early 1780s—to create deep shadows and feathery foliage. Over this, he uses white chalk, which he has wetted for a richer effect, to give a soft light which suffuses and unifies the scene.

Thomas Rowlandson (1756–1827)

The Connoisseurs, ca. 1790

Watercolor, with pen and brown and red ink
9⅜ × 12½ in. (238 × 318 mm.)
Inscribed, center bottom: *the Connoisseurs*

Even in his student days at the Royal Academy, Rowlandson was known for his humorous drawings, and he soon established his reputation as a caricature artist. He satirized every level of society in a prodigious number of drawings and prints, and is invaluable as a social historian of his time. This watercolor pokes fun at art collectors and their taste through the double meaning of the three old connoisseurs admiring a biblical *Susanna and the Elders* in which Susanna is admired and pursued by old men. The figures are vigorously drawn and fully modeled; it is characteristic of Rowlandson's style to suggest solid forms with a few strong, calligraphic lines. This is an early work of about 1790, before his style degenerated into repetitious mannerisms.

Joseph Farington (1747–1821)

Waterfall in the Lake District, ca. 1782

Pen and brown ink, with brown and
grey wash over pencil
24½ × 18½ in. (613 × 470 mm.)

Joseph Farington's reputation derives
more from his diary, discovered in 1921,
than from his achievements as an artist.
The diary is an important record of the
cultural life of London at the turn of
the eighteenth century. Farington was a
prominent figure at that time, a member
of the Royal Academy sufficiently influential to be dubbed "the dictator of
the Academy." He was a pupil of Richard
Wilson and then worked as a landscape
illustrator: many of his watercolors were
reproduced as aquatints in the large
topographical books popular at the time.
One of these, *Views of the Lakes, etc. in
Cumberland and Westmorland*, was first
published in 1789. The watercolor shown
here is more romantic than most of
Farington's work, with its dramatic
waterfall in a craggy gorge. It may have
been exhibited at the Royal Academy
between 1778 and 1782, when all of
Farington's entries were of Lake District
scenes. Two of these were entitled sim-
ply *A Waterfall*, and this drawing may
have been one of them.

Francis Towne (1739 or 1740–1816)

Ambleside, 1786

Watercolor with pen and brown ink
9½ × 6⅛ in. (235 × 156 mm.)
Inscribed, lower left: *F. Towne/delt.
1786 / No 2;* and on verso: *Nº 2 Ambleside
August 7. 1786* and (?) *light from the right* (?)

Although Francis Towne spent most of
his life working and teaching in Exeter,
his finest drawings were executed while
touring Wales (1777), Italy and the Swiss
Alps (1780–81), and the Lake District
(1786). Linear patterns and the defini-
tion of form were Towne's absorbing
interests. His sketches always depend on
the quality of the pen line for their originality and strength. His method, as
demonstrated in this drawing from the
tour of 1786, was to sketch the outlines
on the spot in pencil, and later go over
them with pen and ink, finishing with
flat washes of softly harmonized color.
The composition of *Ambleside* provides
a striking example of Towne's idiosyn-
cratic approach to the formal patterns
created by his subject within the pictorial
space.

John "Warwick" Smith (1749–1831)

Ship in a Bay by Moonlight, 1787

Watercolor

13⅜ × 20 in. (340 × 508 mm.)
Inscribed, lower right: *J Smith 1787*

John "Warwick" Smith received his nickname probably because of his residency in the town of Warwick, although his career was launched by the Earl of Warwick, who financed Smith's study in Italy for five years. Smith traveled and sketched in Italy with Towne and Pars and was much influenced by Towne's style. After his return to England, Smith contributed illustrations to topographical books and in 1792 began publication of his *Select Views in Italy*, containing seventy-two engraved plates. The watercolor shown here is an unusually dramatic example of Smith's work, a romantic moonlit scene reminiscent of Cozens's dark and sublime manner and the nocturnal light effects that interested Joseph Wright of Derby.

North Front of the Hall of Greenwich Hospital.
T. MALTON.

Thomas Malton (1748–1804)

North Front of the Hall of Greenwich Hospital, ca. 1790

Pencil and watercolor
18 × 13¾ in. (458 × 350 mm.)

This watercolor is a good example of the topographical drawings which were a central feature of English art in the eighteenth century. They were intended as an accurate record of architecture and landscape, and the demand for them provided a livelihood for many artists of the time. Thomas Malton learned his skill as a topographical draftsman from his father. When he was established on his own career, he taught drawing and architectural perspective, and Turner was an apprentice with him at one time. In 1792, Malton published a group of aquatints entitled *A Picturesque Tour through London and Westminster*, and the style of this watercolor, with its dramatic use of perspective and clear, accurate drawing, makes it similar to the plates in that publication.

Thomas Girtin (1775–1802)

Warkworth Castle, Northumberland,
ca. 1800

Watercolor
16½ × 21¾ in. (418 × 552 mm.)
Thomas Girtin Collection

Like Turner, Thomas Girtin was trained first in the precise landscape tradition of the topographers and later studied J. R. Cozens's work at Dr. Monro's academy. Although he was only twenty-seven when he died, he had already developed a highly personal and interpretative style which became the progenitor of a large school including J. S. Cotman and Peter De Wint. His method was to build up broad washes of clear color, laying them directly on the paper without making a monochrome underdrawing. This view of the ruins of Warkworth Castle is a characteristic example of Girtin's work just as he was reaching maturity. The somber tones and dramatic low viewpoint link it stylistically to Cozens and the Sublime, but its breadth and rich color sonority mark a departure in the history of watercolor.

William Blake (1757–1827)

Mary Magdalene at the Sepulchre, ca. 1800

Pen and brush with black ink and
watercolor
16⅞ × 12¼ in. (427 × 311 mm.)
Inscribed, lower right: *W B inv*,
monogram

The Bible and Milton were frequently
the sources of inspiration for William
Blake's personal and visionary art; he
also illustrated his own prophetic poems
and that of his contemporaries. Blake
was a professionally trained engraver,
and his art often relies on clear outline
and simple forms with strong contrasts
of light and dark. An example is this
solemn watercolor, where the placing of
the figures of Christ, Mary Magdalene,
and the flanking angels produces a starkly
dramatic design with strong emphasis
on the psychological drama of Mary's
recognition. The watercolor also reveals
Blake's admiration for Michelangelo and
the linear mannerisms of Gothic art. It is
related to a number of drawings illustrating the New Testament which Blake
made in the early 1800s for his patron
Thomas Butts.

Joseph Mallord William Turner, R.A.
(1775–1851)

Lake Geneva and Mont Blanc, ca. 1805

Watercolor and scraping out
28⅞ × 43⅞ in. (734 × 1136 mm.)

Turner's first visit to the Continent in
1802 took him to the lakes and mountains of Switzerland and to the Louvre
and its superlative collection of old master paintings, many of which Napoleon
had looted during his Italian campaigns
of 1796. Turner's paintings, done after
his return to England, reflect the impact
of both these experiences. He made a
long series of splendid watercolors of
Swiss scenes, using an unprecedented,
elaborate technique involving scraping
and blotting out, manipulating the paint
with his fingers, and using saliva. This
large and impressive example is pat-
terned after the serene, classically bal-
anced landscapes of Claude Lorrain and
Nicholas Poussin seen by Turner in the

Louvre; the delicately observed detail
brings the broad shimmering spaces of
Switzerland vividly before our eyes.

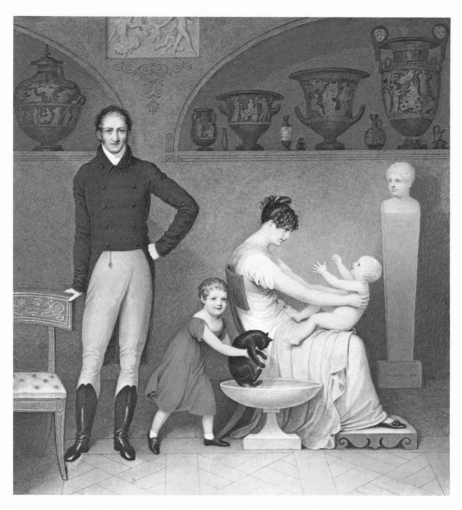

Adam Buck (1759–1833)

Thomas Hope, Designer, and his Family,
1813

Watercolor and pencil
17½ × 16½ in. (445 × 420 mm.)
Inscribed, base of statue at right:
ADAM·BUCK·1813·

Adam Buck was born in Cork but spent
most of his career in London as a miniature and genre painter. The subject of
this watercolor is the family of Thomas
Hope, art collector and author of *House-
hold Furniture and Interior Decoration,*
which was one of the most influential
patternbooks for neoclassical design in
early nineteenth century England. In the
background of this room, a few examples of Hope's important collection of
Greek vases are displayed; some vases
from his collection are now in the Metro-
politan Museum in New York City.
The artist has aligned the figures of Hope
and his children, with his wife turned in
profile, like figures in a classical frieze.
This rather stiff design is enlivened by
the red dress of the child and the delicately modulated way in which the
watercolor medium is used. The Yale
Center for British Art possesses a large
collection of Hope's drawings and
designs.

Edward Francis Burney (1760–1848)

The Triumph of Music, ca. 1815

Watercolor, with pen and black ink
12⅛ × 18⅛ in. (307 × 460 mm.)

Burney made several large drawings of
this sort, satirizing the manners and
pastimes of contemporary society. Here,
the subject is an evening meeting of a
glee club; the numerous inscriptions
scattered throughout the watercolor are
all titles of popular madrigals and
"catches" or rounds. In contrast to the
vigorous style of other satirical artists
such as Rowlandson and Hogarth,
Burney's use of line and contour is very
refined, soft and flowing; subdued color
harmonies contribute to a suave effect.
A study for this watercolor is in the
British Museum.

Henry Fuseli, R.A. (1741–1825)

Ariadne Watching the Struggle of Theseus with the Minotaur, ca. 1815–20

Brown wash and white bodycolor
24 × 20⅛ in. (610 × 500 mm.)
T. E. Lowinsky Collection

Of Swiss birth, Fuseli settled in England in 1772 and became one of the most prominent members of the Royal Academy. During his long career as a successful artist and teacher, he continually drew on Shakespeare, Milton, Dante, and classical myths for inspiration and subject matter. This watercolor illustrates the Cretan legend of the princess Ariadne, promised to the man who could kill the minotaur in the labyrinth of King Minos. It is a good example of Fuseli's extravagant dramatic style, with strong contrasts of light and dark, and exaggerated movements of the figures, and is probably a study for a picture exhibited at the Royal Academy in 1820 and now in a private collection.

David Cox (1783–1859)

Entrance to Calais Harbour, 1817

Watercolor
7⅜ × 11 in. (186 × 280 mm.)
Inscribed, lower right: *D. Cox 1817*

Trained in Birmingham in miniature work and scene painting, David Cox moved to London in 1804. After taking some lessons in landscape, he began to teach himself, a task he humbly continued all his life. During his long career, he made several trips to France, where he produced some of his best work. Cox's ability to render light, wind, and atmosphere is well demonstrated in this delicate watercolor, dated 1817. His first trip to the Continent took place in 1826, and since the subject is identified as Calais Harbor, the date of the drawing creates a problem. Either the date is wrong (perhaps a later addition) or the scene depicted is not Calais, but some unidentified British harbor.

John Constable, R.A. (1776–1837)

Fulham Church from across the River, 1818

Pencil
11⅞ × 17½ in. (300 × 445 mm.)
Inscribed, lower left: *Fulham 8 Sepᵣ 1818*

John Constable, who once wrote that "the solitude of the mountains" oppressed his spirit, was inspired chiefly by the broad open stretches of countryside in and around his native Suffolk. His love for such scenery frequently led him to draw and paint it in the open air. He made numerous sketches such as this one, which shows the Thames near London, using a highly developed pencil technique to capture a great variety of effects of light and texture. Constable notes the exact date and location at the bottom of the sheet; it was probably executed during one of his visits to his wife, who was staying at Putney Heath that summer.

Robert Hills (1769–1844)

A Village Snow Scene, 1819

Watercolor over pencil
12⅝ × 16⅞ in. (320 × 428 mm.)
Inscribed, lower left: *R. Hills 1819*
Thomas Girtin Collection

Robert Hills is primarily known as an accomplished animal painter and etcher. Between 1798 and 1815 he published a series of 780 etchings of animals to serve as embellishments to landscapes, and he was often asked by other artists to enliven their scenes with groups of cattle or deer. He was a founding member of the Old Water-Colour Society in 1804, exhibited repeatedly with this group, and was noted for his fully finished watercolors which could rival the style of oil paintings. In this snow scene, he is able to suggest the textures of wood, fur, straw, and even falling snow, by a stippling use of watercolor and by scratching through the surface. The composition of this watercolor was inspired by the winter scenes of Brueghel, and especially by a Rubens painting of a barn in winter which is now in the Queen's Collection.

Peter De Wint (1784–1849)

A Wagon near a Group of Trees

Watercolor over pencil
8¾ × 11⅛ in. (222 × 282 mm.)

The poet John Clare once begged De Wint for "a bit of your genius to hang up in my cottage . . . one of those rough sketches, taken in the fields, that breathe the living freshness of the open air and sunshine, where the harmony of earth, air, and sky form such a happy unison of greens and greys, that a flat bit of scenery on a few inches of paper appears so many miles." It is a beautiful description of the quality of De Wint's watercolors, of which this study of a wagon and trees is a fine example. De Wint served

an apprenticeship under the engraver, J. R. Smith, and was influenced by Girtin, but soon evolved his own characteristic style of painting with a fully loaded brush, confidently emphasizing the overall masses and contours in his landscapes. He often worked outdoors, completing his watercolors at a single sitting. In this example, he used the motif of silhouetting a detail, the wagon, against a light background, a device used by Gainsborough and other artists of the Picturesque movement.

John Linnell (1792–1882)

Mrs. William Wilberforce and her Child,
1824

Watercolor and bodycolor
14⅛ × 10¼ in. (357 × 260 mm.)
Inscribed, lower right: *by John Linnell
1824*; and lower left: *Water Colors
Mr.ˢ William Wilberforce*
L. G. Duke Collection

John Linnell earned an early reputation
as an able portraitist, particularly of
small-sized portraits, such as this. Later
in his life, Linnell was equally well
known for his landscapes in oil. This
watercolor of Mrs. Wilberforce, the
daughter-in-law of the philanthropist,
William Wilberforce, has an elegance in
the flowing line of her neck and arms
set against a landscape background which
is reminiscent of Renaissance portrait
compositions. The influence of fifteenth
century Italian painting is suggested by
the vivid coloring and by Linnell's ex-
perimental use of the medium, handled
as if it were tempera or fresco. Linnell
was a close friend and patron of William
Blake and father-in-law to Samuel
Palmer.

Thomas Stothard, R.A. (1755–1834)

Scene from Boccaccio's DECAMERON, ca. 1825

Watercolor
10⅝ × 8 in. (270 × 204 mm.)

Stothard executed many oil paintings and made designs for goldsmiths, but his reputation rests chiefly upon his work as a book illustrator. In this field he was prolific, producing graceful watercolors for poetry, prose, and drama with equal facility. His style, influenced at various times by Blake and Flaxman, derives most clearly from the French rococo tradition of Gravelot and Hayman. In this illustration, one of a series engraved for the 1825 edition of Boccaccio's *Decameron*, the artist combines delicate, pretty coloring with a decorative design to create a charming, if unreal, world. It is an anglicized, early nineteenth century version of a Watteau fête galante.

Richard Parkes Bonington (1802–1828)

Seated Woman, ca. 1825

Pencil
7 × 5⅛ in. (178 × 130 mm.)

Richard Parkes Bonington, whose short
career was spent mostly in France, is
best known as a landscape painter. However, along with Delacroix with whom
he shared a studio, he produced numerous figure subjects, mostly of historical
or literary characters. In this drawing
from life, he concentrates on the woman's drapery, and on the play of light
and shadow over the material of her
dress. It is an intimate study, not as highly
finished or as artificial as his historical
costume pieces, but it displays his crisp,
firm, and authoritative draftsmanship.
Bonington's work was very much admired on the Continent; it influenced
Boudin and, through him, the French
Impressionists.

Samuel Palmer (1805–1881)

Cornfield and Church by Moonlight,
ca. 1827

Pen and ink, with brown wash
heightened with white
6 × 7¼ in. (152 × 184 mm.)
T. E. Lowinsky Collection

Like William Blake whom he admired, Samuel Palmer was a visionary artist and frequently found inspiration in the Bible, Milton, and classical literature. This brooding drawing was done early in Palmer's career, when he was living in the village of Shoreham, Kent, which he later called his "valley of vision." These Shoreham drawings were not ex-hibited in Palmer's lifetime but are today his most admired works. They interpret the English countryside in a richly ima-ginative, highly personal way. Palmer's work for the remainder of his career was more conventional, but in his later years he took up etching, and his late prints often recapture the romantic sensitivity of these early drawings.

John Sell Cotman (1782–1842)

A Summer Day, ca. 1832

Watercolor
12½ × 18½ in. (318 × 469 mm.)
Inscribed, lower left: *J. S. Cotman*

John Sell Cotman found it difficult to earn his living as an artist; his career was dogged by financial crises which forced him to teach and undertake the exhausting task of illustrating books on architectural antiquities in order to survive. Cotman received some training in London and was influenced by the watercolor style of Girtin; however, he lived in Norwich most of his life, where he was a leading member of the Norwich Society of Artists. This watercolor is apparently a view of Postwick Grove, on a bend of the River Wensum near Norwich. Cotman's style is characterized by unusual clarity of design and a highly individual concept of form. The brilliant color of his later watercolors, as in this example, increases the abstract quality of his designs.

Thomas Shotter Boys (1803–1874)

The Church of St. Magnus by London Bridge with the Monument, 1832

Watercolor over pencil
13¾ × 10⅝ in. (348 × 271 mm.)
Inscribed, lower right: *Thos Boys. / 1832.*

Thomas Shotter Boys was trained as an engraver in England and went to Paris when he was twenty to seek employment. There he met Richard Parkes Bonington and was influenced by his fluid, virtuoso manner of painting watercolors. Boys adapted this style to his landscape and architectural views of France and Belgium. He learned lithography while in France and in 1839 published *Picturesque Architecture in Paris, Ghent, Antwerp, Rouen, etc.*, a lavish "coffee table book" of its time with fine color lithographs based on his own watercolors. It was followed in 1842 by *Original Views of London As It Is*, a group of monochrome lithographs printed in sepia. This watercolor view of London illustrates Boys' style of combining a spacious architectural scene with groups of figures and unifying the whole with a lively play of light and shade.

William Henry Hunt (1790–1864)

Birds Nest and Apple Blossoms, ca. 1850

Gouache
10 × 12⅛ in. (255 × 307 mm.)
Inscribed, lower left: *W. Hunt*
Thomas Girtin Collection

William Henry Hunt concentrated in his later years on still life studies and became well known and admired for his skills in reproducing the textures of fruit, vegetables, leaves, etc., in his work. He began his career as a landscape and genre painter, and by 1824 was a member of the Old Water-Colour Society. A few years later he stopped painting in oils and turned to watercolor. The example shown here illustrates Hunt's particular technique of using an underpainting of Chinese white mixed with gum to which he carefully added bright, opaque color. Thus his works have a heavy, almost tactile quality, well suited to his humble subjects. Hunt's work was admired by John Ruskin, who praised his faithfulness to nature and mastery of detail.

Sir John Everett Millais, P.R.A.
(1829–1896)

Accepted, 1853

Pen and brown ink
9⅞ × 6⅞ in. (250 × 175 mm.)
Inscribed, lower right: *John Everett Millais/1853*; lower left: *to be painted moonlight*; and center bottom: *Accepted*
Verso: pencil drawing of a woman and child

This drawing is one of a group dealing with contemporary social subjects which Millais executed in the early 1850s. A companion sheet, also at the Yale Center for British Art, is entitled *Rejected*. Both are drawn with a fine pen in a style characteristic of drawings made at that date by all the members of the Pre-Raphaelite Brotherhood, of which Millais was a founder.

The artist's note at the bottom left indicates that he considered using the subject for a painting. The motif of embracing lovers recurs in his work of this period from *A Huguenot* of 1852 to the *Black Brunswicker* of 1860. On the reverse of this sheet is a pencil study of heads for Millais's picture *The Order of Release, 1651*, which was shown at the Royal Academy in 1853.

John Frederick Lewis, R.A. (1805–1876)

Roman Pilgrims, 1854

Watercolor and bodycolor
22⅛ × 30⅜ in. (560 × 770 mm.)
Inscribed, lower left: *J F Lewis. 1854.*

Lewis's father and uncle were both artists, and young John Frederick had an
early success with his animal paintings
and prints. His extensive travel in Europe
and the Near East—he lived for ten
years in Egypt—provided him with subject matter for the remainder of his life,
and he became famous for his meticu-
lously detailed, richly colored paintings
of exotic subjects. This example shows
his method of using opaque bodycolor
to achieve solid areas of bright color with
an enamel-like richness. The myriad

details of carpet, windows, altarpieces,
and costume effectively convey the lav-
ishly ornamented and sunlit interior of a
Roman basilica, and are typical of
Lewis's sumptuous effects.

Liber · xij ·

Incipit liber · xij. de Auib9 in generali et speciacili. Ca · J

Or the treatife is ended of the proprytees of the ayre and of thynges that ben gendryd therin / Jt is couenable to this prefent volume to treate of

fome thynges whiche bylonge to the worthyp ⁊ magnyfyfence of god. in whiche thynges the meruayllous ⁊ excellent dedes of the Creatour maye be praysid as of otherthynges / To the ornamement of the ayre bylongen byrdes ⁊ foules as Beda fayth'/ And therfore by the helpe of p̃ goodnes of Jhefu Cryft. fomwhat of them fhall be treated confequently in this boke · Not of all. but oorly of fuche byrdes ⁊ foules whiche ben fpecially fpo

Wynkyn de Worde (d. 1534)

Headpiece to Book XII, "De Avibus in generali et speciacili" from *De proprietatibus rerum*, by Bartholomeus Anglicus. Westminster, ca. 1495

Woodcut
11¾ × 9¼ in. (29.7 × 23.3 cm.)

Printing was introduced to England in 1476, about twenty years after its invention in Germany, by William Caxton, a Kentish mercer who had learned the art in Cologne. It was probably in Cologne that he enlisted the services of Wynkyn de Worde, his first apprentice. After Caxton's death in 1491, de Worde inherited Caxton's premises in Westminster as well as all his equipment. In contrast to the early presses on the Continent, Caxton and de Worde concentrated on printing books in the vernacular, which were assured a ready audience among the merchants and professional men of London. *On the nature of things*, by Bartholomeus Anglicus (fl. 1230–1250), was an encyclopedic compilation of natural history as medieval man knew it. The version here illustrated, printed by de Worde in 1494 or 1495, is of the English translation made in 1398 by John of Trevisa. Each of the nineteen books, or chapters, treats a major division of natural history, and is headed by an illustration of that branch. Here the subject is bird life; the illustration, while recut from a Flemish original, captures a love for nature and animals so prevalent in later English art, especially in the paintings of Francis Barlow.

Robert Adam (1728–1792)

"Design of a Ceiling in the Etruscan taste executed in the Countess of Derby's Dressing room." Plate VII, part 1, volume II of *The Works in Architecture of Robert and James Adam*. London, 1779

Engraving
25⅝ × 19½ in. (65.2 × 49.5 cm.)

Interest in the use of classical motifs in architectural decoration received impetus from excavations carried out on classical sites in Italy and Greece during the eighteenth century. Perhaps the most astonishing discovery of the century was that of the villas buried in Pompeii and Herculaneum, where domestic interiors were preserved intact underneath volcanic lava. Herculaneum was one of the sites Robert Adam visited in 1755 while on his Grand Tour; there and elsewhere in Italy, he developed a love for classical architecture, especially Roman domestic

interiors and newly discovered Etruscan ornamentation. In his own work as a domestic architect, he sought to employ a classical vocabulary of ornament with greater freedom than revivals of earlier times had done: freedom in the use of these motifs, he felt, was closer to the true spirit of Roman architecture than slavish imitation of surviving monuments. Adam was the first modern architect to adapt Etruscan motifs to domestic decoration, as he points out in his commentary for this illustration, executed in 1773–74.

Jean François Albanis Beaumont
(1753?–1811)

"Southern View of the Col de Tende."
Opposite page 39, in *Travels Through the
Maritime Alps*. London, 1795

Sepia aquatint
18⅛ × 12⅜ in. (46.2 × 31.5 cm.)
J. R. Abbey Collection

Towards the end of the eighteenth century, the love of travel, already manifest
in the popularity of the Grand Tour,
acquired fresh characteristics from its
association with the new interest in
picturesque scenery (see also p. 93).
Books illustrating the picturesque scenery to be found on the Continent, particularly along the Rhine or the Loire,
or in the Alps, proliferated for an ever-
widening audience. Among the earliest
of these books were those produced by
Albanis Beaumont, a native of the Pied-
mont who became naturalized in England ca. 1790. He was at once a landscape painter, draftsman and engraver,

although the illustrations for this book
were engraved from his designs by
Cornelius Apostool. Alpine scenes, with
irregular mountain profiles and precipi-
tous drops into caverns or rushing rivers,
owed some of their popular success to
the taste for "Gothick" novels set in
such locales.

Nikolaus Willem von Heideloff
(1761–1838)

"Bathing Place." Figures 151–52,
volume IV of *The Gallery of Fashion*.
London, 1797

Hand-colored aquatint
11¾ × 9½ in. (29.7 × 24.2 cm.)
J. R. Abbey Collection

There was an enormous outburst of costume books in England from about
1790 onward, illustrating both the cos-
tumes of faraway places and historical
eras, as well as the latest fashions at home.
Many collections of these "fashion
plates" were merely ephemeral, but some,
like Heideloff's *The Gallery of Fashion*,
are notable for the spirited, lively scenes
evoked to depict the fashions. Heideloff,
a German born in Stuttgart, had gone
to Paris in 1784 to continue his artistic
studies, and fled to England at the time
of the French Revolution. In London
he worked for Rudolph Ackermann, one
of the great publisher-entrepreneurs
who exploited the possibilties of color-
plate books. *The Gallery of Fashion* began
monthly publication in April 1794, and
was completed in nine volumes in 1802.
Many of the plates illustrate not only
the new fashions of the classical revival,
characterized by high waistlines and
clinging drapery, but also fashionable
watering spots of society. In the plate
illustrated here, the two modish young
women stand on a bluff overlooking the
beach of a seaside resort: bathing ma-
chines are to be seen on the lower left.

Fig. 151.   *Fig. 152.*

Published as the Act directs, Sept.r 1797 by N. Heideloff at the Gallery of Fashion Office, N.o 90 Wardour Street.

Drawn & Engraved by T. Medland, Abingdon Str. Westm.

TEMPLE OF BRITISH WORTHIES.

Published July 17 1793 by J. Seeley, Buckingham.

Thomas Medland (d. 1833)

"Temple of British Worthies." Opposite page 21 in *Stowe: A Description of the House and Gardens*, published by J. Seeley. Buckingham [1797]

Engraving
10⅜ × 7⅞ in. (26.4 × 20 cm.)

The gardens at Stowe House, Buckinghamshire, were the inspiration of Sir Richard Temple, Viscount Cobham (1669–1749), a Whig statesman and owner of the estate. He employed, successively, the architects Vanbrugh, Bridgeman, Gibbs, Kent, and Capability Brown in laying out the grounds and designing numerous small buildings which dot the landscape. The distinctive feature of the gardens is the iconographic program: the layout of temples and monuments was calculated to produce associations with classical antiquity, the Middle Ages, and British history, all tied together by the theme of English freedom. The various shrines commemorate heroes of republican liberty, seen as forerunners of the Whig leaders of eighteenth century England. The climax of the theme occurs in the Temple of British Worthies, here illustrated across a picturesque prospect. Designed by William Kent (1684–1748) in 1733, it was intended as a miniature national portrait gallery, its classical architecture meant to associate the national heroes depicted with the Roman republic. The gardens of Stowe quickly became a popular excursion site, much as country houses are today. Guide books such as this one were published both as souvenirs of a visit and for explanation of the landscape program.

Thomas Bewick (1755–1828)

"Red-Legged Crow" and Winter
Vignette. Pages 118 and 119, volume I
of *The History of British Birds*. 2d ed.,
Newcastle, 1804

Wood engraving
9½ × 5¾ in. (24 × 14.8 cm.)

Thomas Bewick, animal artist and wood
engraver, was a native of Newcastle-
upon-Tyne, where he spent most of his
working life and established a new school
of wood engraving. The technique of
woodcut for book illustration had de-
clined by the eighteenth century, and
was used only for cheap, popular books
of ballads or children's stories. Bewick
developed an improved technique using
the end grain of the wood, which en-
abled wood engravings to rival the work
of copper plate engravings, but left
them suitable for use in more modest
books. His work evidences not only
technical mastery of engraving, but also
the keen observation and feeling for
English rural life of a lifelong country-
man. *The History of British Birds* was one
of a celebrated series of books describing
the animals of England, illustrating them
in small, affecting images like that of
the crow shown here. Scattered throughout the text of these books are tailpiece
genre vignettes touchingly evocative of
the rustic scene, like the boys depicted
here setting up a snowman.

THE RED-LEGGED CROW.

Plate V.

5　　　10　　　15

J. Clark del.　　　Published Sept.r 1.t 1807, by Edw.d Orme Bond Street, London.　　　J. Hamble sculp.

John Heaviside Clark (ca. 1770–1863)

Plate V (untitled landscape) from
*A Practical Essay on the Art of Colouring
and Painting Landscape.* London, 1807

Hand-colored aquatint
15⅝ × 10⅞ in. (39.7 × 27.6 cm.)

The popularity of watercolor painting, particularly for rendering landscape scenes, grew not only among professional artists, but also among amateurs. A knowledge of watercolor painting became a requisite accomplishment of any educated gentleman or lady. Hence the best professional teachers were much sought after, and many of them propounded their methods in treatises intended for those who could not procure a private tutor. A great outpouring of such manuals began to appear around the turn of the nineteenth century, the best of them the serious output of watercolor masters like David Cox, Samuel Prout, and John Varley. This book by John Heaviside Clark was the first of the genre to use the reproductive technique of aquatint for printing the illustrations, aquatint being especially suitable for reproducing the tonal variations found in watercolor paintings. It depicts a landscape scene to be copied by the pupil; different plates show various stages in the production of a finished work: outline, shading, coloring. In the plate illustrated, color samples are provided at the bottom of the picture to guide the pupil in preparing and mixing colors.

William Gilpin (1724–1804)

"Scaleby Castle." Plate 20 from
Observations on Several Parts of England.
3d ed., London, 1808

Tinted aquatint
8⅞ × 5¾ in. (22.7 × 14.7 cm.)
J. R. Abbey Collection

The Reverend William Gilpin, school-master brother of the animal painter Sawrey Gilpin, was an important figure in the development of the taste for Picturesque landscape. From 1769 he undertook travels to scenic parts of England and Wales, recording his impressions in a series of *Picturesque Tours*, published from 1782. He set out to define and illustrate from nature those features which constitute the Picturesque as a mode of beauty, in contrast to other concepts prevalent at the time, like the Sublime or the Beautiful. According to Gilpin, the Picturesque was characterized by irregular features: jagged crags, bent tree limbs, and especially ruins of ancient buildings such as that illustrated here, of Scaleby Castle in the Lake District of

Cumberland. His books had enormous success, stimulating not only a torrent of published Picturesque tours both in Britain and abroad, but also a steady stream of parodies such as Combe and Rowlandson's tours of "Dr. Syntax."

CHINESE LADY.

Drawn & Engraved by Thos & Willm Daniell.

Published by Messrs Longman Hurst Rees & Orme, Paternoster Row, July 1 1810.

Thomas Daniell (1749–1840) and
William Daniell (1769–1837)

"Chinese Lady." Plate 29 from
*A Picturesque Voyage to India by the
Way of China.* London, 1810

Hand-colored aquatint
10½ × 14⅛ in. (26.6 × 36 cm.)

The popularity of Continental tours had
a vicarious counterpart in the interest
in reading about journeys to exotic
Asian and Antipodean countries. Thomas
Daniell, a landscape painter, and his
nephew William went on an explora-
tory expedition to the interior of India
in 1784, remaining there for ten years
and visiting sites previously unexplored.
Upon their return they produced several
publications of scenes of India, as well as
this smaller work which describes the
places, primarily in China, visited en
route to India. The illustration repro-

duced here typifies their careful interest
in reporting the costume and manners of all walks of life encountered: the
woman shown is described in the text
as a "lady of quality" and her daily
activities are enumerated and contrasted
with those of other classes of women and
men. The Daniells' accurate as well as
beautiful reportage was the first major
break with fanciful impressions of sup-
posed Chinese views which had earlier
proliferated amidst the taste for chi-
noiserie.

SOUTH SIDE OF KING'S COLLEGE CHAPEL.

Frederick Mackenzie (1787–1854)

"South Side of King's College Chapel."
Opposite page 204, volume I of
A History of the University of Cambridge,
published by Rudolph Ackermann.
London, 1815

Hand-colored aquatint
15 × 12¼ in. (38 × 31 cm.)
J. R. Abbey Collection

One of the most successful series of publications produced by Rudolph Ackermann, the foremost publisher of color-plate books in early nineteenth century England, was that illustrating the universities of Oxford and Cambridge. The plates were issued in monthly parts from 1813 to 1814, accompanied by a narrative history of the universities and their constituent colleges. The great success of these plates was due only in part to their appeal to the nostalgia of old graduates; the depiction of antique architecture in settings conforming with the canons of the Picturesque lent them more general appeal. Mackenzie was one of the artists who provided the designs for a large number of the plates; he had begun his career as the pupil of an architect, and as a draftsman he specialized in conscientious drawings of ancient buildings, particularly ecclesiastical structures. The Chapel of Kings College, Cambridge, is perhaps the most spectacular building in either of the universities, a magnificent example of the latest Perpendicular phase of Gothic architecture.

Gothic Hall

HAMPTON COURT.

Charles Wild (1781–1835)

"Gothic Hall, Hampton Court."
Opposite page 32, volume II of
The History of the Royal Residences,
by William Henry Pyne. London, 1819

Hand-colored aquatint
14¼ × 11¾ in. (36.2 × 30 cm.)

William Henry Pyne (1769–1843), a watercolorist by training and early practice, later devoted himself to designing, engraving, and writing. *The History of the Royal Residences* was his most ambitious effort, containing in two volumes one hundred colored aquatints of Windsor Castle, St. James's Palace, Carlton House, Kensington Palace, Hampton Court, Buckingham Palace, and Frogmore. Pyne wrote the text for the sumptuous book, but the illustrations were all drawn by other artists, most noteworthy among them Charles Wild. Wild was an architectural painter, a pupil of Thomas Malton (who was also Turner's teacher), from whom he acquired a feeling for the spirit as well as the appearance of Gothic architecture. This view of the interior of the Gothic Hall at Hampton Court is successful not only in depicting the architectural details of the structure, but also, through its near emptiness, in conveying a sense of the antiquity and bygone glory of Henry VIII's great palace, no longer the home of the monarch.

Designd & Etch'd by D.T. Egerton.

There are some Men in the world who cannot confer a slight favour on you, without considering themselves entitled to claim an intimacy with you at any period however distant, & under any circumstances however mal a-propos. To have a Leech of this description (to whom the fates have since proved unkind) attach himself to you on any of the fashionable promenades, is unbearably Boring, as it exposes you to be quizzed and cut by all your acquaintance.

Daniel Thomas Egerton (d. 1842)

"The Leech." Plate 2 from *Fashionable Bores, or Coolers in High Life*, by Peter Quiz [*sic*]. London, 1824

Hand-colored aquatint
11⅜ × 15¼ in. (29 × 38.8 cm.)
J. R. Abbey Collection

Among the many classes of illustrated books which proliferated in the nineteenth century was that devoted to caricature and parody. While political caricatures, usually in the form of separately issued prints, had been popular throughout the eighteenth century, caricatures of fashionable society only began to appear at the end of the century, at the same time that social satire appeared in the novels of Henry Fielding, Fanny Burney, and Jane Austen. Among the artists whose caricatures were issued in books were Thomas Rowlandson, James Gillray, and Pierce Egan.

Egerton was better known as a land-scape painter, but he published two volumes of social parody, *Fashionable Bores* and *The Necessary Qualifications of a Man of Fashion*. As in the plate illustrated, his barb was usually aimed at foppish dandies whose main concerns in life were to be fashionably dressed and present a proper outward impression to others with similar taste, frequenting the right clubs and coffee houses. From the caption to "The Leech" it is hard to tell who is more the butt of the joke: the leech himself, or the narrator who is so concerned about how he appears to others during the confrontation.

John Whittaker (fl. 1823–1830)

"The King's Herbwoman with her Six Maids." Plate 5 from *The Coronation of George the Fourth*, published by John Whittaker and George Nayler. London, 1821–41

Hand-painted stipple and line engraving, on vellum
30¼ × 25⅛ in. (77 × 63.8 cm.)
J. R. Abbey Collection

The coronation of George IV was a great spectacle, a daylong event marked by all the pomp and grandeur befitting the investiture of the man who had led England's society as Prince Regent for more than a decade prior to his formal accession. The splendor of the proceedings was recorded in a great many paintings, prints, panoramas, and sumptuous illustrated books. Perhaps the most luxurious of the books was that begun by John Whittaker in 1823, with text printed in gold letters, and many of the portraits finished in oil colors and varnishes. All told, Whittaker published over forty plates depicting in detail the dignitaries present at each stage of the ceremony. One of the more delicate illustrations is that of the procession shown here, of the King's Herbwoman, Miss Fellowes, with her own train of attendants.

The copy of the book in the Yale Center for British Art is a unique copy intended for presentation, perhaps to George IV himself, although he died before the work was completed. It is printed on vellum and silk and ornamented with gold braid and jewels, and bound in a highly decorated heraldic binding.

Samuel Prout (ca. 1784–1852)

"Verona." Opposite page 19 of *The Pictorial Album, or Cabinet of Paintings,* by George Baxter. London, 1837

Chromo-xylography
10 × 7⅝ in. (25.3 × 19.3 cm.)

Samuel Prout was one of the many topographical artists who started their careers by drawing the illustrations for John Britton's eighteen volume work, *The Beauties of England and Wales* (1801–15). In 1818 he visited the Continent, and subsequently became best known for his views of foreign cathedrals and marketplaces; this view of Verona is typical in its romantic image of a foreign city. The reproduction of Prout's watercolor in *The Pictorial Album* is interesting, too, as an early example of color printing by a woodblock technique perfected and promoted by George Baxter (1804–1867). Unlike most earlier book illustration where the color was either applied by hand or else consisted of only one or two tints, Baxter printed all the colors mechanically, sometimes employing as many as twenty different blocks for each final print.

Philip Brannon (fl. 1850–1870)

"Gate to Hyde Park," "The Crystal Palace," and "View of the Serpentine." Title page of *The Park and the Crystal Palace.* London, 1851

Chromolithograph
23⅝ × 17⅞ in. (60 × 45.4 cm.)

The Great Exhibition of 1851 was the first international exhibition of arts and manufactures—direct ancestor to the present-day World's Fair. Under the patronage of Prince Albert, the enterprise was planned to include every type and process of manufacture and handicraft from around the world, to be assembled in a great exhibition hall in Hyde Park. The Crystal Palace, as the glass hall became known, was designed by Joseph Paxton (1803–1865) and covered nineteen acres of the park, enclosing within it live trees. The appeal of the exhibition and the palace to all classes was immediate and phenomenal: the exhibition not only fulfilled its stated aim of stimulating trade and design, but also contributed a new purpose to excursion travel. Elaborate catalogues were available to the visitor, illustrating both the phenomenon of the Crystal Palace as well as the objects of art and industry on view. Unofficial productions such as Brannon's book, here illustrated, were intended more as picturesque souvenirs of a visit than as informative guides.

Design & Typography
Howard I. Gralla
New Haven, Connecticut

Composition & Printing
The Press of A. Colish
Mount Vernon, New York

Binding
Publishers Book Bindery
Long Island City, New York

Production Supervision
Yale University Printing Service